FLYING ON INSTINCT

Canada's Bush Pilot Pioneers

L.D. CROSS

HERITAGE

VICTORIA · VANCOUVER · CALGARY

Heritage House Publishing Company Ltd.
heritagehouse.ca

CATALOGUING INFORMATION AVAILABLE FROM LIBRARY AND ARCHIVES CANADA

978-1-927051-84-9 (pbk)
978-1-927051-85-6 (epub)

Series editor: Lesley Reynolds
Proofreader: Liesbeth Leatherbarrow

Cover photo: "Bob Cockeram's Noorduyn Norseman MK II *Ruth IV*," by Robert W. Bradford, courtesy of Canada Aviation and Space Museum, Ottawa.

The interior of this book was produced on 30% post-consumer recycled paper, processed chlorine free and printed with vegetable-based inks.

We acknowledge the financial support of the Government of Canada through the Canada Book Fund (CBF) and the Canada Council for the Arts, and the Province of British Columbia through the British Columbia Arts Council and the Book Publishing Tax Credit.

Canada | Canada Council for the Arts | Conseil des arts du Canada | British Columbia | British Columbia Arts Council An agency of the Province of British Columbia

20 19 18 3 4 5

Printed in Canada

Contents

Prologue

THE PILOT WAS IN SERIOUS TROUBLE. *The charter flight had started out well, roaring off into sunny skies en route to a remote northern fishing lodge. As a bush pilot, he had made hundreds of these routine trips carrying prospectors, campers, mail, food, and on one journey, four sled dogs and their musher. But this time his engine had conked out at 5,000 feet (1,524 metres) and would not sputter back to life no matter how much he coaxed and cajoled it. He was losing altitude fast and had to find a place to put down. Where were all those smooth lakes and big rivers when you needed them? Even a sandbar would be welcome. But there was not a clearing or bit of scrubland to be seen—only the endless evergreen forest below. A crash landing was inevitable, but where? His two passengers, who at first had enjoyed the soft, quiet glide after the engine cut out, were now well aware of the danger and too terrified to scream. They sat hunched down in their seats, hoping for the best, which obviously was not going to happen.*

Trying to keep his nose up and the plane as level as possible, he spied a grove of young trees that were thinner and less dense than the big spruces growing all around. He aimed for that spot and went in nose first, trying to maintain as much control as possible and pointing the engine between the trees. If the main body of the plane could just slide in and not hit a tree trunk head-on, maybe he and his passengers would survive. The small plane shuddered, and the landing gear ripped off as soon as it hit the treetops. Branches beat against the underside of the fuselage, but at least that slowed them down a bit. The plane dropped but kept moving forward at an alarming speed. All the pilot could see was green coming at him and rapidly flashing past his shoulders. His passengers saw nothing at all because their eyes were clamped shut and their heads were between their knees. The propeller disintegrated into lethal shards that flew back, shattering the windshield and banging into the thin skin of the fuselage like exploding bits of shrapnel. The wings were long gone, sheared off by tree trunks that tore huge chunks out of the frame. Miraculously the cockpit and cabin compartments were still intact, but the fuselage was now a violent projectile careening through the forest.

The occupants were forcefully thrown around inside what remained of their capsule. They had tightened their lap belts and shoulder harnesses on the way down, more as a useless gesture toward convention than in any hope that it would keep them safe. Arms, legs and heads smashed around as the bashed-up box they were riding in turned on its side and skidded to a stop against a tree root in an unrecognizable heap. Even the registration markings were gone. The engine that had caused their wild ride was rammed under the cockpit. Pieces of wing and other debris were strewn in the trees and along the ground for over a kilometre. The air reeked of fuel, but fortunately there was no fire.

The pilot painfully turned around and looked back. One of the passengers was dragging himself out of the open cabin. The other slumped motionless over the side. They were bloodied and bruised with multiple broken bones, but all three were alive. Now all they could do was to wait to be rescued.

CHAPTER

1

Up and Away

BUSH FLYING BEGAN IN CANADA. Almost 8 percent of the country is water, a natural landing site for bush pilots and their float planes in summer. In winter, the frozen surfaces made excellent landing strips for planes equipped with skis. Otherwise planes were set down on snowy tundra or makeshift landing strips in the middle of nowhere.

Bush flying created the gateway to the riches of the North and the means to get there. There was scarcely a place in the country where bush pilots would not go, and every remote region had an independent air operation and service facilities to keep it flying. Forty-five–gallon fuel drums were stashed at trading posts along the way or left at a wilderness cache. It was a different time, and pilots were a different breed. They were the off-roaders of aviation. Yet even today, some small, remote Canadian communities still rely on bush planes and the intrepid pilots who fly them to bring in everyday necessities that residents in the south take for granted.

Before the First World War began in 1914, Canada had few pilots or planes. After the war ended in 1918, one-third of Britain's Royal Flying Corps (RFC) was composed of Canadian pilots who had volunteered to serve king and empire. Flying had previously been the rare pastime of the rich or reckless, but during the war the RFC was the preferred choice of soldiers wanting lift off into clean, open skies and escape the cold, muck, gas and vermin-infested confines of the trenches. Their getaway vehicle was a flimsy wood-and-cloth airplane.

This trade-off was not always a good one. There were no parachutes, and the fuel tanks were located under the seat. If his aircraft caught fire during an aerial battle, the pilot had three very bad options: ride the plane down and hope to survive the crash; jump out and face inevitable death; or grab his service pistol and shoot himself. The average lifespan of a First World War fighter pilot was 17 flying hours. The RFC was dubbed "the suicide club."

Some soldiers were encouraged by their superiors to transfer to front-line flying because they were considered problematic misfits. Alan Duncan Bell-Irving of the Gordon Highlanders, for example, was ordered by his company commander to apply for a transfer (which was immediately approved) because a group of generals had seen him standing behind a berm wearing only his shirt and boots. He had removed his kilt to burn off the lice. As a pilot, Bell-Irving went on to earn the Military Cross for gallantry in action and much later to attain the rank of air commodore in the Royal Canadian Air Force (RCAF) during the Second World War.

After the signing of the armistice with Germany in 1918, some military pilots returned to Canada looking for opportunities to use their flying expertise in civilian life. Surplus airplanes were readily available. A Curtiss JN-4 Canuck could be had for the equivalent of $1,200, but airfields were scarce, and most aviators were skilled flyers, not mechanics. Maintenance was a problem and crashes were frequent. Governments were disinterested in funding a permanent military air force. After all, hadn't the First World War been "the war to end all wars"?

One of those returning military pilots was William George "Bill" Barker. Barker was born in a log house near Dauphin, Manitoba, in 1894 and as a teen loved horseback riding and shooting. His sharp eyesight and steady hand made him a crack marksman. In December 1914, in his final year of high school, he enlisted in the First Canadian Mounted Rifles. He was sent to France as a machine gunner, then transferred to the RFC. Returning to France as a fighter pilot, he shot down 50 enemy aircraft in sorties from 1916 to 1918, finally sustaining severe injuries to his legs and also to his left elbow, which essentially made him a one-armed pilot. Awarded many honours, including the French Croix de Guerre and the British Victoria Cross, his luck finally ran out. He crashed his Sopwith 7F.1 Snipe, but while recuperating in London, he met fellow Victoria Cross recipient William Avery "Billy" Bishop.

Back home in Canada by 1919, the pair formed Bishop-Barker Company Limited, one of Canada's first commercial air services. In a race from Toronto to New York and back, Barker became the first Canadian pilot to carry international airmail, and in 1921, the first to fly commercial cargo between the US and Canada. But like many other flying ventures, the company was ahead of its time; it ceased operations in 1922. Barker went back to the military, joining the new Canadian Air Force (CAF), then resigning in 1926 and taking a series of unsatisfying jobs until becoming vice-president of Fairchild Aircraft Ltd. in Canada. On March 12, 1930, while demonstrating the new Fairchild KR-21 biplane trainer at Rockcliffe air station, he lost control and was killed when his plane struck the ice of the Ottawa River. Obscured by the fame of Bishop, who outlived him by almost three decades, Barker remains Canada's most decorated war hero and proved there was a non-combat role for larger-than-life flyers employing their military skills in civilian work.

Major W.G. "Bill" Barker, wearing goggles and a flying helmet, pilots Fokker D.VII aircraft No. 50 during the air race between Toronto and New York in 1919. LIBRARY AND ARCHIVES CANADA C-014058

Arthur Massey "Matt" Berry, a farm boy from just outside Ottawa, was commissioned at the outbreak of the First World War and transported overseas. He was then transferred to the RFC. After the war, he became a civilian flying instructor, eventually getting a commercial pilot's licence in 1928. Berry got a job at Northern Aerial Mineral Exploration Ltd. and was the first pilot to land at Baker Lake, Northwest Territories. In 1921, he became the first pilot to fly round trip between Great Bear Lake, Northwest Territories, and Edmonton in the same day. Berry joined Canadian Airways Ltd. as a pilot in 1931 and was instrumental in saving the lives of many people stranded in the Arctic wilderness.

In 1935, Berry located and flew to safety downed CAL pilot Con Farrell and his air engineer F. Hartley, who had been stranded for 11 days on the Barrens after a blizzard forced their plane down. The next year, Berry was again a hero when he rescued RCAF flight lieutenant S. Coleman and leading aircraftsman J. Fortey from north of Great Slave Lake, then led a record-breaking mission with his air engineer, Rex Terpening, to rescue Bishop Falaise and his party, who were stranded by a blizzard at the Roman Catholic mission at Hornaday River above the Arctic Circle. Persevering through darkness and blinding snowstorms, Berry and Terpening located the group and returned to bring them food, only to be grounded themselves for 10 days before flying everyone out safely. Until this exploit, no aircraft had ever flown that far north during the winter.

Air engineers like Terpening sat in the right-hand cockpit seat on daily flight operations. They refuelled the aircraft, fixed any structural damage, repaired the engine and even warmed the oil so the engine could start on cold winter days. And they did it all in remote locations with basic tools, using only their innate innovative abilities and courage to resurrect broken aircraft so they would fly again.

In 1942, the US government recognized Berry's expertise in Arctic transportation and hired him to oversee construction of airfields in the Northwest Territories and the CANOL (Canadian Oil) Project, a pipeline and road system to supply fuel for the military during the Second World War. In the

A contrast in winter modes of travel by air and land, Matt Berry's aircraft spreads its wings beside Richard Finnie's traditional dogsled and team in Coppermine, Northwest Territories, in 1931.
LIBRARY AND ARCHIVES CANADA PA-100602

post-war period, he and partner Max Ward developed Yellowknife Airways Ltd., then Berry went on to found Territories Air Services Ltd. at Fort Smith before turning to northern mining ventures. Ill health forced his retirement in 1969; he died the following year in Edmonton.

Wilfred Leigh Brintnell was another First World War flyboy, joining the RFC in 1917 and then becoming an instructor with the RAF the following year. After the war, he looked for other opportunities, but it was not until 1927 that he began working for Western Canada Airways (WCA). Brintnell completed a 9,320-mile (15,000-kilometre) flight in a Fokker tri-motor aircraft inspecting WCA sites from Winnipeg north through the Northwest Territories to Great Slave Lake, then from the Mackenzie River to Fort Norman.

From there, Brintnell flew north to Aklavik on the Arctic Ocean. The next leg of his flight was the first across-the-Rockies flight from Aklavik to Dawson City, Yukon. From there he proceeded to Prince Rupert, on British Columbia's Pacific coast, returning back to Winnipeg via Edmonton. In 1932, Brintnell formed his own company, Mackenzie Air Service Ltd., in Edmonton and began flying passengers on regular schedules and charters across the Northwest Territories and Arctic until his airline was sold and amalgamated into Canadian Pacific (CP) Airlines in 1940.

In 1929 Brintnell made a historic flight that helped fuel the atomic bombs dropped over Japan to end the Second World War in 1945. Mining entrepreneurs Gilbert LaBine and Charles St. Paul were aboard when Brintnell made the first flight completely around Great Bear Lake. During the flight, the excited passengers caught sight of what appeared to be signs of silver and pitchblende, indicating uranium deposits, around the shoreline. Back on land, LaBine rushed to stake a claim, and Eldorado Mines Ltd. was in business. The largest deposit of uranium ore in the world, Eldorado produced radium salts, a market then monopolized by Belgium, for medical rather than military use.

On March 19, 1935, six years after that first flight with LaBine, Brintnell and co-pilot Stan McMillan took off from the mine in a Bellanca Air Cruiser with the initial shipment of radium concentrates on board. Later, in 1942, the US government ordered some 220 tons of uranium ore from

Leigh Brintnell poses with Bellanca 66-70 Air Cruiser CF-AWR of Mackenzie Air Service Ltd. in Edmonton in 1935.
LIBRARY AND ARCHIVES CANADA PA-015652

Great Bear Lake to fuel experiments in the Manhattan Project, so Eldorado ore was used in the first chain-reaction experiments to produce a nuclear bomb. LaBine signed a supply contract after scientists discovered the ore contained high levels of uranium oxide, a nuclear-energy source. But it wouldn't last. The Eldorado mine at Port Radium, Northwest Territories, was secretly expropriated and ownership transferred to the Canadian government in 1944. The company was nationalized as a crown corporation and renamed Eldorado Mining and Refining Ltd. Uranium ore from the mine was used in the secret laboratories of the Manhattan Project at Los Alamos, New Mexico, to fuel the first atomic weapons, named Little Boy and Fat Man, dropped on Hiroshima and Nagasaki—all this from a charter flight around a lake in the Northwest Territories.

CHAPTER

2

From War Birds to Wilderness Wings

IN 1919, ELLWOOD WILSON, a forester with Laurentide Pulp Company in Quebec, came up with the idea of using airplanes to spot forest fires long before they became huge infernos that could destroy large swaths of valuable timberland owned by Laurentide and other pulp and paper companies. Planes also provided the sweeping aerial views that made photographing and mapping timber holdings much easier. But the new flying machines were scarce and very expensive. However, in a post-war gift, Wilson found out that the US Navy was declaring its wartime Curtiss HS-2L coastal patrol flying boats as surplus. The Canadian government was the lucky recipient of 12 of these flying boats. Wilson asked for the loan of two of them, and hired Captain Stuart Graham, just returned home from the Royal Naval Air Service (RNAS), along with his engineer, Bill Kahre, to fly the first one up from Halifax-Dartmouth, Nova Scotia, to Grand-Mère/Lac-à-la-Tortue, Quebec. Graham agreed, but with reservations.

The Curtiss was not a sleek flying machine, but it had a lot of character. It was noisy, and when its Liberty engine overheated, boiling water from the radiator spewed over cabin occupants. Pilots said it resembled a pelican with big biplane wings mounted high over a thick, bathtub-shaped fuselage. In bad weather, it took the muscle power of both the pilot and his engineer to grab the controls and keep their bird aloft. Manoeuvring on water was even more problematic. Often the engineer had to climb out onto the lower wing so his extra weight would force either the right or left wing-tip float into the water to allow the pilot to turn in toward a dock or out onto a lake. It could be capricious—sometimes choosing to start and sometimes not—and sometimes demanding immediate mechanical adjustments either while airborne or while dead in the water amid swirling clouds of blackflies and mosquitoes.

The Curtiss flying boat's wooden hull absorbed water, which added weight and reduced the amount of cargo it could haul. Often bad weather or engine breakdowns forced the HS-2L onto the nearest lake, regardless of the lake's size. Airmen soon discovered that seaplanes need more room to take off than to land, so a pilot had to use ingenuity to get airborne again. They used several techniques. One such technique was to attach a rope to the plane, tie it around a convenient tree and then rev the engine. When the engine was at full power, the engineer leaned out and cut the rope so the aircraft would slingshot into the air in a shorter distance. Also, because of the plane's unique wide hull, pilots could get up to takeoff speed in one direction, then make a sharp turn at the end of the lake and have enough momentum to clear trees or rocks at the other end of the lake. But then again, sometimes the engineer had to chop down those pesky trees along the line of liftoff. Pilot, engineer and passengers all sat in open cockpits and faced rain, snow and skin-searing cold. Then there was winter ice. The HS-2L was a flying boat, not a skier, and as soon as ice formed over a lake, it was grounded until spring. But in spite of these handicaps, the Curtiss HS-2L was Canada's first bush plane. It was big enough to carry five people or their equivalent weight in cargo and could land on just about any body of water. All it needed was a fearless pilot and an agile engineer to manually manoeuvre it as required and provide ongoing TLC.

Stuart Graham, Canada's first professional bush pilot and a member of Canada's Aviation Hall of Fame, began his civilian career in a Curtiss HS-2L called *La Vigilance*. Graham's wife became the first Canadian woman to help crew a plane when she travelled with him between Nova Scotia and Quebec. After a few days in Halifax familiarizing himself with his awkward airship, Graham took the Curtiss HS-2L flying boat on her maiden flight back to Quebec. A crew of three—Graham as pilot, his wife, Madge ("Poppy"), as navigator, and Bill Kahre as engineer—flew the aircraft at treetop level from Nova Scotia to Quebec. The HS-2L had only rudimentary instruments: a compass, an air- and wind-speed indicator and a turn-and-bank indicator. The noise from the engine made conversation impossible, so Madge strung up a miniature clothesline to send written messages to and from the occupants. The flight took four days in June and covered 645 miles (1,038 kilometres), the longest cross-country flight in Canada at the time. The crew then returned to Halifax-Dartmouth and delivered the second HS-2L to Quebec.

Everything was set for the first summer of bush flying doing aerial photography and fire patrols along the St. Maurice River valley. Using the two flying boats, patrols were extended from Lake of the Woods (Lac des Bois) in Ontario to James Bay. This continued for two summers, but by 1921, operating costs were so high that the Laurentide Company refused to fund the patrol-only pursuit any longer and reorganized it into Laurentide Air Service Ltd. with Ellwood Wilson as president and barnstormer William R. Maxwell as vice-president.

Looking for financial support, Maxwell convinced Quebec shipbuilder Thomas Hall to invest $10,000 to create a commercial arm of the business. In the summer of 1922, Laurentide carried 310 passengers during 688 flying hours

A handling party launches Curtiss HS-2L flying boat G-CYDS of the Canadian Air Board from the dock at Victoria Beach, Manitoba, in 1921. LIBRARY AND ARCHIVES CANADA PA-05328

as a bush charter service for prospectors, hunters and lumbermen. Based on this success, Maxwell bought 12 more HS-2Ls sight unseen. Many were still in their factory shipping crates. He hired six pilots who flew mapping expeditions covering 20,000 square miles (51,800 square kilometres) of forest in Ontario. In 160 flying hours they mapped an area that would have taken ground surveyors five or six years to cover.

The government of Ontario took note and created its own Ontario Provincial Air Service (OPAS), poaching Maxwell and other staff away from Laurentide along with many of its customers. In one 1926 operation, OPAS planes flew 27 men and 6,420 pounds (2,912 kilograms) of equipment to successfully fight a remote northern forest fire that could not have been extinguished any other way. "No man," Maxwell said, "approached or left it by ground." Backed by public funding from the Ontario government, OPAS lived on into the 1940s while Laurentide died in 1925 from the loss of key personnel and business to OPAS. Laurentide missed the Red Lake gold rush by mere months.

In the summer of 1925, Lorne and Ray Howey discovered gold under the roots of an upturned tree at Red Lake in the Canadian Shield. When news of the discovery reached the outside world in March 1926, dogsleds mushed over frozen wilderness and bush planes buzzed overhead in the wildest stampede since the Klondike gold rush of 1897–98. In one hour, a plane could cover an area that would take 12 days to travel by land. More than 3,000 men trekked up the frozen Hudson River for six days and nights in bone-freezing cold to reach the Red Lake base camp. From there, they still had to survive staking and working a claim. In 1934, the price of gold rose from $20 to $35 an ounce, resulting in increased mining activity in Red Lake.

The Red Lake gold rush proved the usefulness of the float planes that would soon dominate northern transportation. Early on, the Red Lake Transport Company had used 60 teams of horses for hauling winter freight, and sternwheel barges, tugs and freighter canoes in summer to help get fortune seekers in. Faster modes of transportation were needed to get their gold out to southern buyers. In 1927, Red Lake was the service centre for prospectors, miners and construction crews working at the Howey Gold Mine. Ten years later, Howey Bay in Red Lake was an air hub for planes of all types, on skis or floats, with payloads of people and cargo arriving and departing at 15-minute intervals. At the height of the gold-rush staking period, this bush-plane airport without radios or a control tower was the busiest airport in the world!

The Canadian-designed and built Noorduyn Norseman fulfilled the miners' needs and more. In 1935, Dutch-born aircraft designer and manufacturer Robert B.C. Noorduyn decided to build a bush plane for Canadian conditions. To get it right, he asked bush pilots what they needed. They told him that the plane must have high wings so they could see where they were going, and four doors, two on each side, so they could load and unload large cargoes quickly. Whatever cargo wouldn't fit inside, such as canoes or lumber, could be balanced and strapped to the wing struts or floats for transport. The plane had to be easily adaptable to floats, skis or fixed-wheel landing gear. It had to be rugged enough to withstand rough water in summer and plow through snowdrifts in winter. And speaking of winter, it had to have an insulated cabin and heated cockpit.

The 10-passenger Norseman was the ideal bush plane—sturdy, reliable and easy to repair. It was also used for troop transport during the Second World War. The designation "Norseman V" was reserved by the company until the end of the Second World War to represent Winston Churchill's "V for Victory" symbol. Until 1953, the Canadian military used the Norseman as light utility transport, then replaced it with the de Havilland Otter. When production ended in 1959, a total of 903 Norsemen had been built. In the 1960s, over 20 Norsemen were still stationed in Howey Bay servicing the North. Some are still flying, most in Canada.

A Norseman (USAAF tail number 44-70285) gained some infamy when it disappeared over the English Channel on December 15, 1944, while carrying famous American bandleader Glenn Miller en route to Paris to join his Army Air Force Band. No trace of the plane was ever found, but its flight plan was through an area used by returning B-17 bombers to jettison unused bombs after a mission. It is speculated such a bomb hit Miller's Noorduyn UC-64A Norseman, which was at a lower altitude. RAF pilot Fred Shaw reported that a small plane was seen crashing into the North Sea near that route, but the mystery surrounding the death of Glenn Miller and the two crewmen has never been conclusively solved.

One of the new air services formed to take advantage of business opportunities in the goldfields was Patricia Airways and Exploration Ltd., named for the district in which the lake was located. Its head pilot, Harold Anthony "Doc" Oaks (both his father and his uncle were doctors and the family may have wanted to steer him in that direction) was a former captain in the RFC, a geologist and a mining engineer with a degree from Queen's University. Oaks decided that flying to the digs was more profitable than prospecting them. He sold his claim and rented an HS-2L, plus a tiny Curtiss Lark biplane with two open cockpits, one for himself as pilot and one that held up to 400 pounds (180 kilograms) of mining equipment or two passengers snuggled tightly together.

During 1926 and 1927, Oaks and his Lark, equipped with floats or newfangled skis, made up to 10 trips a day carrying a total of 260 passengers, as well as 14,000 pounds (6,350 kilograms) of prospecting gear and 3,000 pounds (1,360 kilograms) of mail to Red Lake, Ontario. Profits soared. The Lark was cheaper to operate than the heavy HS-2L, so Oaks decided to form a new air service with light, agile planes. He tapped James A. Richardson, a Winnipeg grain exporter, for funding, and they formed Western Canada Airways Ltd., a commercial aviation company that began with a fleet of exactly one Fokker plane. Oaks did double duty as pilot and business manager, Al Cheesman was the mechanic and J.A. MacDougall their head office clerk. The plane bore the registration G-CAFU and the name *City of Winnipeg*.

The company serviced mining camps and did it so well that they won a major contract from the federal government to airlift drilling machinery, surveyors and engineers to

Hudson Bay. The plan was to move western wheat through Manitoba to a rail terminus in either Port Churchill or Port Arthur, but only if the bay at either town could be dredged deep enough to handle huge grain ships bound for Europe. Both ports were ice-free in summer, but only drilling would determine if the geology was suitable. And it had to be done quickly. Rail crews would finish the Hudson Bay Railway line next summer. Could Oaks do it now? He knew winter flying in the North would be difficult, but this was a once-in-a-lifetime opportunity.

With Richardson's money, Oaks bought three Fokker Universal planes and hired three pilots: two RFC veterans poached from OPAS and skilled Norwegian cold-weather aviator Bernt Balchen, who had participated in Arctic air searches for lost polar explorers. When he first sighted his new employer's headquarters, Balchen could not believe his eyes. "It was little more than a lean to," he wrote in his diary, with "an impressive sign over the door: Western Canada Airways." But it was a multi-purpose lean-to, comprising "ticket office, freight station, and passenger terminal for the whole flying gold rush" he noted. The Fokkers arrived from the American factory, and they were in business.

The Fokker Universal was the first aircraft built in the US based on the designs of Dutch aircraft designer Anthony Fokker, who had worked for Germany during the First World War. About half of the 44 Universals built between 1926 and 1931 were used in Canada and flown by legendary bush pilots like Walter Gilbert and Punch Dickins. While the Curtiss HS-2L flying boat could only operate in summer, the Fokker had an interchangeable undercarriage and could be outfitted with floats, wheels and skis for virtually all-season operation. Fokker established the Atlantic Aircraft Corporation at the Teterboro Airport in New Jersey to build other aircraft under licence.

In 1926, Fokker made plans to create a sturdy civilian aircraft designed to land on very rough airstrips, or none at all. One of the features that made this possible without shaking the plane apart was an early shock absorber made of bungee cord. The new plane, the Fokker Super Universal, evolved from the Fokker Universal under design refinements spearheaded by Robert Noorduyn, who would later build his own Noorduyn Norseman bush plane. The mixed-material construction consisted of a welded steel-tube frame for the fuselage, fabric-covered tail surfaces and a plywood wing with a span of 47.74 feet (14.55 metres) mounted above the fuselage. It had a single 149 kW (200 hp) Wright J-4 radial engine and later a 246 kW (330 hp) J-6 engine. Two gasoline tanks were mounted in the wings, and at a maximum speed of 118 MPH (190 Km/h) it had a range of 535 miles (860 kilometres). The pilot sat in an open cockpit forward of the wing's leading edge. The enclosed cabin below and to the rear of the pilot held four to six passengers or was fitted for cargo estimated up to 940 pounds (427 kilograms).

In 1927, a Fokker Super Universal sold new from the

factory for $14,200. But on March 31, 1931, the wing of a Trans World Airlines (TWA) Fokker fell off during a flight between Kansas City and Los Angeles. The plane crashed, killing all on board. The American government decreed all future passenger planes must have two engines and be made of metal. William Boeing and Donald Douglas began building such planes, and Anthony Fokker's company was acquired by North American Aviation in 1933.

On March 23, 1927, the first major flying project at Western Canada Airways (WCA) got underway when two open cockpit Fokkers piloted by Bernt Balchen and Fred Stevenson picked up 1,200 pounds (544 kilograms) of drilling equipment from the end of the rail line at their Cache Lake, Manitoba, base and deposited it at Port Churchill. The Churchill Operation, as the press dubbed it, was the first time large amounts of cargo had been airlifted into the Canadian Arctic.

On one return trip, Fred Stevenson failed to show up. Seventy-five miles (120 kilometres) north of Cache Lake, his oil line burst and he put down on a frozen lake. With darkness falling, Stevenson snuggled into his flight suit and went to sleep with howling wind and wolves for company. At sunrise, he spotted fresh footprints and followed them to a cabin. The Native occupant was startled by the unexpected company, but he and Stevenson agreed on a price for a dogsled, and Stevenson mushed south. The dogs, however, weren't up to the trip, so Stevenson released the tired animals and continued on alone through thigh-high snow. Meanwhile, Balchen and his engineer, Al Cheesman, had taken off at first light in search of their missing friend. They spotted the downed plane but not Stevenson. Planes were too expensive to be left sitting on a remote lake, so they decided to land and fly it out. Cheesman, who had some flight experience, got the engine going and took off. When he saw the low oil-pressure gauge, he set the plane back down, fixed the broken line and made it back to Cache Lake with Balchen following in the other Fokker. When Stevenson finally got back to base after three days of slogging through snowdrifts, the first thing he saw was the plane he had left back at the lake, now sitting on the landing strip. He truly thought he had been out in the bush too long.

On a subsequent takeoff, Stevenson ripped his undercarriage, but the only place where repairs could be made was at a train depot 135 miles (218 kilometres) away. He piled the broken parts onto a railway handcar, and with Cheesman pumping one handle and Stevenson the other, they seesawed their way there and back.

Balchen had his adventures, too. Caught in a blizzard near Eskimo Point, Manitoba, as the sun was setting, he decided to land on snow-covered tundra and wait out the storm. He was rocked to sleep by strong winds pummelling his plane but was roused in the early morning darkness by a peculiar bumping motion. Trying to focus through the dim light and blowing snow, he could just make out a big white shape. A polar bear was butt to butt with the back end of his plane, using the horizontal stabilizer as a scratching post. Balchen decided to let the itchy bear be; however, before taking off into a clear sky the next morning, he made a careful inspection of the aircraft's tail section.

In spite of such contretemps, by April 22 eight tons of equipment and 14 workers had been delivered to Port Churchill. Balchen noted that on their last takeoff from Cache Lake, there was so much water on the melting ice that the ski-fitted Fokkers resembled seaplanes.

The 1927 Churchill airlift for the Hudson Bay Railway was the first of its kind in Canada, and probably the world. It was successful at a time when aviation and northern flying were far from mature, and when communication and navigation aids were primitive at best. It's therefore a tribute to the determination and skill of all concerned. The Department of National Defence said: "The decision during 1927 as to the selection of Fort [Port] Churchill as the ocean terminus of the Hudson Bay Railway was made possible by these flights. There has been no more brilliant operation in the history of commercial flying." The completion of this project established the usefulness of aircraft in remote areas, not only in mining and geologic surveys, but also in servicing distant communities. Equally important, it established WCA as a pioneer in northern aviation.

Following the successful Churchill Operation, WCA founder Doc Oaks moved on to other accomplishments, launching Northern Aerial Mineral Exploration Ltd. to fly mining engineers and prospectors into remote locations from Hudson Bay to the Rockies to sample Precambrian rocks that yielded gold, silver, nickel, zinc and copper. He established fuel depots across northern Canada so flights could go farther in greater safety. To ease winter engine start-ups, he and Cheesman developed small heated tents called "nose hangers" that fit over engines and allowed work to be done without frostbitten fingers. In January 1929, WCA established a regular air service along the Mackenzie River to Fort McMurray.

In 1927, Oaks became the first recipient of the McKee Trophy for achievement in aviation. Known as the Oscar of Canadian aviation, the McKee Trophy (Trans-Canada McKee Trophy) is the oldest aviation award in Canada. It is given annually to a Canadian whose achievements have been "most outstanding in promoting aviation in Canada." It was donated by Captain J. Dalzell McKee, an American pilot who completed the first seaplane flight across Canada from Montreal to Vancouver in a Douglas MO-2B in 1926, accompanied by Squadron Leader Earl Godfrey of the RCAF.

Oaks was inducted into Canada's Aviation Hall of Fame, which is located in Wetaskiwin, Alberta, in 1974, with the following commendation: "The professional daring of his aerial expeditions into uncharted regions led others of his breed to colonize the unknown north and bring outstanding benefits to Canadian aviation."

CHAPTER

3

Winged Workhorses and Flying Canoes

BUSH FLYING INVOLVES OPERATIONS in all weather conditions and terrain—over desert, tundra, mountains, forest, water, and snow and ice with short, makeshift landing strips or no landing strips at all. In 20th century Canada, any sparsely settled region outside the narrow band of development near the US border was called the boonies, the backcountry or the bush. Sometimes it still is. There were roads and railways along the southern boundary and coastal transportation by boat, but the boreal Canadian Shield and the remote Arctic tundra were uncharted and undeveloped wild country accessible only by canoe, horseback or dogsled. Bush planes would become the 20th-century equivalent of the fur-trade voyageur's canoes.

Today, flight training is available to qualify for a pilot's licence and certification, but pioneer pilots had no bush-flying instruction. They adapted their military flying skills to the new environment and learned by doing. If they did well, they survived. They flew by visual flight rules (VFR) following ground reference markers such as rivers and avoiding obstacles like mountains, clouds and other aircraft. Some joked that IFR meant I Follow Rivers, instead of instrument flight rules, where the pilot uses cockpit instruments and electronic signals. Sometimes they sketched what they saw, and these crude maps became the only rudimentary charts available. Large sections of Canadian government maps had no reference points and were identified with the disconcerting notation "unmapped." When they flew into uncharted areas, pilots would pick out landmarks, then try to find them in reverse order on the way out—it was easier said than done. A pilot could land and take off at numerous lakes or clearings in a day's work, moving along an erratic course that was difficult to replicate. Often, a pilot found the best way out was by straight-line flying by "the seat of his pants" back to a reference point his compass and instincts told him should be there. Homing pigeons and bush pilots had a lot in common. There was no Global Positioning System (GPS) or air-traffic controller to assign routes and altitudes. Pilots were on their own.

Bush planes were, and still are, equipped with floats, skids, skis or tires (and the ability to switch as conditions change) depending on the intended route. They must have short takeoff and landing capability (STOL), which is defined as the ability to take off and clear a 50-foot (15-metre) obstruction in a distance of 1,500 feet (457 metres) from beginning the takeoff run, plus the ability to stop within 1,500 feet after crossing a 50-foot obstacle on landing. There is no margin for error in clearing trees on takeoff or avoiding the shoreline on landing.

Typically, bush-plane wings are on top of the fuselage to prevent them from hitting the lumps, bumps and bushes in the landing area. The undercarriage, or landing gear, supports the aircraft on the ground and is of two main types. Conventional or taildragger undercarriages are configured with two wheels toward the front and a single, smaller wheel or skid at the rear. Tricycle or nose-wheel undercarriages have two main wheels under the wings and a third smaller wheel under the nose.

In early aviation, the taildragger arrangement was preferred since it allowed greater propeller ground clearance to avoid hitting rocks and deadheads (submerged tree stumps or trunks); however, it required greater pilot skill to land and take off because any deviation from a straight trajectory amplified drag and could make the aircraft unstable since the main wheels were forward of the plane's centre of gravity. The tricycle arrangement had tail-strike problems (the plane's rear end would hit the runway) if the pilot pulled up too quickly or raised the nose too sharply during landing. In the case of a taildragger undercarriage, the tail was already on the ground with a wheel or skid underneath. In the tradeoff that is bush flying, the taildragger aircraft has better aeronautic ability, but the tricycle type can land almost anywhere if equipped with oversized tires. The skill of the pilot was, and is, the most important factor in flying either type of aircraft.

Bush flying was hard physical labour, too. After putting down in a remote location, the pilot had to unload the plane, usually by himself. The ground was rough and rock-strewn, or spongy muskeg and muck. If a pilot was lucky, when he landed on water he could pull up to a dock, but often he had to wade into the water, pull the cargo out piece by piece, carry it to shore and then scramble up an embankment through thick underbrush to high ground.

The early planes used for bush flying were adapted from military uses and not specifically designed for ferrying freight in the Far North. However, the post–First World War slump in military aircraft sales motivated manufacturers to look at new designs and new markets. Bush planes were a profitable niche. British, American, European and Canadian designs took to life in northern skies. Names like Bellanca, de Havilland, Fairchild, Junkers, Norseman, Stinson and Vickers became recognizable names in bush flying. Ironically, veterans of the First World War who turned to bush flying in civilian life were confronted with a descendant of their nemesis—the Red Baron's Fokker Dr.1

triplane—when the Fokker Universal and later the Super Universal became popular bush planes.

The Junkers Flugzeug- und Motorenwerke AG (JFM), commonly known as Junkers, was a major German aircraft manufacturer that pioneered all-metal aircraft also used in bush flying. Its model Junkers W33 was a single-engine transport aircraft, aerodynamically advanced for the 1920s, a low-wing, all-metal cantilever monoplane. It holds a place in aviation history for making the first east-west, non-stop, heavier-than-air crossing of the Atlantic. The Junkers W34 was developed from the W33 and carried a pilot and five passengers or their equivalent weight in cargo. The Junkers were nicknamed "flying boxcars" because they were capable of delivering large loads inside their square fuselage. And the low-wing design was a welcome safety feature for pilots landing on thin ice. If the skis broke through, the broad wings kept the passenger and cargo compartment up out of the water, at least for a while.

The small used planes that flew in the North went through many crashes, hard landings and makeshift mends; one pilot referred to his craft as little more than "a collection of spare parts." Those parts had to hang together over huge uninhabited areas. Despite these significant equipment problems, the greatest challenge to the early airborne surveyor, fire spotter or photographer was the immense size of the country. Even by the start of the Second World War in 1939, large tracts north of the 57th parallel (roughly on a horizontal line above current day Fort McMurray, Alberta) were still unmapped. In 1920, the new Canadian Air Force (the Royal label was added in 1924, removed in 1968 and reapplied in 2011) was tasked with surveying Canada by air. It was to be a straightforward operation: fly a continuous line, without deviation, back and forth over unmapped areas while a photographer busily took multiple overlapping photos that would be pieced together in a topographical map by cartographers. But the project did not go smoothly. Minor turbulence caused the early light planes to bump around, and variations in altitude distorted the map scale, making ponds and ridges smaller or bigger as the plane moved up or down. The mere dip of a wing shifted the scale sideways. Clouds blocked visibility and eliminated great swaths of territory below. It was said of the eventual result that "the only good thing about those charts was the price—25 cents."

No obstacle was more irritating to early Canadian bush pilots than freezing temperatures. Winter flying required patience and perseverance. Parked outside in sub-zero weather, everything froze solid. At -40°F/C this happened in less than an hour. It was the job of the flight engineer, or the pilot if he was flying alone, to prep the radial internal combustion engine for shutdown and start-up. Every night the oil was drained into buckets and brought into the cabin or tent, and if possible, the engine was covered by a canvas tarp draped over the nose and propeller as slight protection from the biting wind and snow. The next morning, they set to work in the pre-dawn darkness, because pilots wanted to lift off at sunrise to maximize daylight flying hours. The oil was warmed in a double boiler to prevent scorching (which ruined its lubrication ability) on a wood stove or fire right along with breakfast. While this was underway, the engine was prepped by warming with a kerosene heater called a blow pot for at least an hour. (Blow pots were originally designed for melting lead used by plumbers working with metal pipes before plastic pipes were readily available.) The thinned oil was carefully poured back into the warmed engine, which the pilot prepared to start. If it did not turn over, the problem had to be found and corrected before everything froze solid again. If a pilot failed to follow the warming routine, he went nowhere. A frozen engine was dead, and encouraging it back to life was slow, dangerous labour. The air reeked of gas fumes as the blow pot roared into action, and without careful attention, it could set the entire wood and fabric plane on fire. More than one blow-pot blow-up grounded pilot and passengers—and incinerated the cargo. If that happened, the best hope was that someone would see the smoke from the man-made torch and fly in for a rescue. Otherwise it was a long walk to civilization or a long wait until spring thaw. After use, the blow pot was stowed in the tail section of the plane, ready for the next night.

By the late 1930s, the US Air Force began to thin circulating oil with gasoline in order to get northern fighter aircraft airborne faster without preheating engines and oil. Canadian Airways of Winnipeg had a winter fleet of 40 aircraft, and its president, James Richardson, authorized a trial installation. If the new technique worked, the cost savings and safety benefits would be huge. It did work, but single-plane operators continued to use the blow pot at northern locations.

A large part of the time spent bush flying went to preparing the plane for flight, rounding up the passengers and loading and securing the cargo. Even then, things could go wrong. Sometimes a plane's skis were frozen to the ground. One approach to freeing them was to rev the engine at full tilt while your helpful engineer, a passenger or a local resident grabbed the plane's tail, bounced it up and down and shook it from side to side. While doing this, the helper was being blasted by pieces of ice thrown back at high velocity in the propeller slipstream. That was if a pilot was lucky enough to have a helping hand; if he didn't have a human agitator, he could try jumping on the skis to loosen the icy grip or pour warm water over them. Leftover breakfast coffee might do the trick or maybe peeing on them would help.

Winter was not the only season fraught with challenges. In summer, fog or rain could sweep in quickly, and pilots had to decide whether to drop down so they could still see ground markers, risking a crash, or climb higher but lose visibility and risk becoming lost. Even the finest flying weather could be dangerous. Mirror-smooth lake water perfectly reflects the sky and causes pilots to become disoriented, unable to determine how high they are above the lake's surface. The calm conditions known as glassy water are the most deceptive phenomenon known to the float pilot and make it difficult to judge the final few feet. Landings take a considerable distance, so the worst-case scenario is a heavily loaded aircraft landing on a short lake in glassy conditions. A glassy water takeoff can be equally unnerving, as the surface of the water is very hard to discern. A fixed reference point like a rocky outcrop, point or dock helps in calculating distance.

Spring and fall, the "changeover" seasons when ice was melting or water was freezing, were also dangerous. Bush pilots had to guess whether they needed wheels, floats or skis, and what was needed for takeoff was often not appropriate when and where they landed. Granular old snow called firn tended to suddenly break under pressure and grab sinking skis. New snow drifted and hid obstacles like rocks, fallen trees and stumps. Either situation could cause a nasty crash. Pilots who survived a crash were faced with the challenge of repairing their plane thousands of miles from help. Fortitude and ingenuity were all that mattered.

In the mid-1920s, two pilots with Canadian Airways broke a propeller blade during a hard landing on crusted snow at Fort Smith, Northwest Territories. The closest replacement was in Buffalo, New York. No problem. They bought a wooden sled and a moose hide from Natives and set to work using basic items from the small onboard tool kit. With a knife, they shaved strips of hardwood off the sled then boiled up bits of hide in water until all that remained was a gelatinous glue that would stick the wood strips together. Using small files and eyeballing the dimensions, they crafted a handmade prop that got them back to base in Fort McMurray, Alberta. Flying home was the easy part.

When not flying, pilots were known to party hearty, especially during long winter nights when fewer flights were scheduled. In one 1925 incident at the Boiler Room Bar in Sault Ste. Marie in northwestern Ontario, a mock trial was staged when a young pilot was accused of wearing his flight suit, leather helmet and goggles into the bar with the sole intent of impressing the ladies and "attracting advances by the fair sex." The accused explained to the moot judge and jury, composed of fellow pilots who were sitting in judgment on his crime, that he had done so simply to keep warm and that alcohol had not been involved in his sartorial choice that night. In fact, he said, he had consumed alcohol only once in his entire life and had never been drunk. The entire barroom-cum-courtroom was filled with jeers and shouts of "That's what's wrong with him!" Following the obvious verdict of guilty, the judge delivered his horrible sentence: barred from the bar for two weeks. Then everyone lifted a glass or more of distilled beverage to toast the swift application of frontier justice.

CHAPTER

4

Airborne Exploration

THE GREAT AGE OF BUSH FLYING and aerial exploration in Canada coincided with the launch of the Fairchild FC-1 all-purpose aircraft. Before starting production, the manufacturer in Long Island, New York, had asked bush pilots what characteristics they wanted in the planes they flew, then incorporated those recommendations into the first models. Pilots wanted a high-wing monoplane so they could easily see the ground. They also wanted an air-cooled radial engine to eliminate the irritating cold-weather problems caused by the liquid-cooled engines in the many war-surplus planes that were still in use. But most of all they wanted an enclosed, heated cockpit and cabin. And so in 1927 the purpose-built FC was born: F for Fairchild and C for closed. It featured fabric-covered metal-tube construction for ease of repair and innovative hinges at the base of the wings so they could be folded for storage. The Fairchild could be outfitted with wheels, floats or skis for year-round flying. It was smaller, faster and easier to fly than the open cockpit Fokker but carried an equal payload. In short, the Fairchild was ideal for bush flying and its design features were much copied by other manufacturers.

Exploration and development were the catalysts for flights into the West and North. Small bush planes took mere hours to travel to and from remote communities that previously had been accessible only by foot, horse, boat or sled. Pilots developed their own flying techniques to land on sandbars, Arctic ice floes and rocky Barrens. They became a vital part of everyday life and transformed the expectations of northerners in the 20th century. It was possible to charter an aircraft and fly almost anywhere. Air transport became affordable to trappers and missionaries, geologists and surveyors. The ill and the injured could be evacuated quickly for medical attention. Bush flying in support of mining operations even continued through the Great Depression of the 1930s, when more freight was being moved by air in Canada than in all the rest of the world combined. Tales of bush pilots' fascinating adventures began growing as fast as stories about their wartime air-combat sorties.

In August 1929, Lieutenant Colonel C.D.H. MacAlpine,

the president of Toronto mining company Dominion Explorers, set out for the high Arctic with eight engineers and prospectors in two single-engine planes. The expedition members intended to stake claims in a rich copper field that was to be opened to public development by the Canadian government. They used MacAlpine's own Fairchild FC-2 and leased a Fokker Universal from WCA. Dominion's pilots had started venturing into the North on exploratory mineral-seeking flights.

This time, MacAlpine planned a three-week sweep of the Northwest Territories to the Arctic Ocean, but the group ran into bad luck and challenging weather. At the start, one plane was lost at Port Churchill when a high tide in Hudson Bay swept it away. The replacement arrived a week later, but the delay proved costly. When they finally got underway, their compasses were affected by the north magnetic pole; seriously off course, they hit bad weather, ran out of fuel and made an emergency landing at Dease Point, in what is now Nunavut. Stranded over 100 miles (160 kilometres) inside the Arctic Circle, they hunkered down beside their float planes and figured out where they were.

At this time, planes were not radio-equipped, and there were only six radio stations in operation across the territories, so no one knew of their predicament. The group decided to sit tight until freeze-up, then walk out over the ice. They figured correctly that the nearest white settlement was at Cambridge Bay, where the Hudson's Bay Company

(HBC) had a post on Victoria Island off the northern mainland. To reach Cambridge Bay, they would have to walk 60 miles (97 kilometres) west along the coast, then traverse 25 miles (40 kilometres) of still-open ocean to Cambridge Bay. But first they had to wait for the water to freeze. They settled in beside an Inuit hunting camp where they constructed a 4-foot-high by 12-foot-long (1.2 by 3.7-metre) shelter of stone, mud and moss roofed with canvas from a tent that kept blowing off in the strong winds. Food and ammunition were strictly rationed. Each person got two meals a day. Hunting parties amassed a stockpile of ptarmigan and ground squirrels, while gathering teams collected moss and willow twigs for fuel. The Inuit supplied them with 55 dried whitefish (which the stranded explorers ungraciously deemed "awful greasy") and 2 dried salmon. On October 15, the temperature dropped well below zero, and the Inuit at the camp indicated that they could walk out soon.

On October 21, they struck out northwest along the coast. With Inuit guides and three sled-dog teams they climbed over rough pack ice, weaving in and out of coastal ice floes in -25°C (-13°F) temperatures. The Inuit built snow igloos each night, and they dined inside on boiled trout and salmon supplemented with bacon and sugar from their dwindling emergency rations. Seven days later, they started across the frozen Victoria Strait. A quarter of the way across they were stopped by open water. There was nothing to do but go back. Six days passed, and only dog food remained. The men began to fight among themselves. One of the expedition's pilots, Stan McMillan, wrote, "It has often been said that even among the most enlightened peoples of this earth, the veneer of civilized behaviour is thin. We didn't suffer any conspicuous peeling of this veneer, but incidents did occur where one might say fractures developed."

The Inuit had left to resupply the group and returned on November 1 with caribou, fish, flour, sugar and tobacco. The next day, the MacAlpine group set out again, threading a course across ice floes. Sled travel was difficult as they had to shove the sleds over huge hummocks of ice without losing their footing. When they hit areas of thin ice the Inuit tested it with their spears. If it withstood a sharp throw, the chances were that it would hold a man, at least for a short time. November 3 was the final and most fearsome day of their trek. In a -27°C (-17°F) wind chill, they fanned out across undulating sheets of ice, running fast and avoiding darker patches that indicated very thin ice or open water. As they ran, they could hear the crack and groan of moving ice sheets, but they all made it across and staggered into the HBC post on November 4. All they wanted were clean clothes, dry footwear and food. The post manager used old wireless equipment on board the ship *Bay Maud* to send the message "all well" down south. The men were amazed that they were now in better physical condition than when they flew out on their expedition. There was only one permanent injury among them; one man had three toes amputated because of frostbite. They all agreed that without the help of the Inuit they would have died on the tundra.

Had all gone well, the MacAlpine expedition would have been back home by September 20. When they had failed to show up at Bathurst Inlet on the Arctic Ocean, 360 miles (580 kilometres) northeast of Yellowknife, by September 24, one of the few northern radio stations sent out word that the group, due 12 days earlier, still had not arrived. An aerial search started that day. For eight weeks, bush pilots flew over 30,000 square miles (77,700 square kilometres) of Arctic Barrens, battling fog, mist, rain and snow, navigating by the sun or the seat of their pants when their compasses were disturbed by the nearby north magnetic pole. The rescuers also became stranded at remote locations when fuel was low, food scarce or equipment broke. It was one of the largest aerial searches in Canadian history to that date.

The world press was fascinated and, according to MacAlpine's grandson, "gobbled up every detail of the search" for the missing prospectors. Finally, the search was called off when word came that the MacAlpine expedition was safe. Lieutenant Colonel MacAlpine and his mining associates footed the cost of the search, which was almost $400,000. During their ordeal, the stock market crash of 1929 happened, and a journalist noted, "Such investors as were on board the two aircraft who had left a buoyant, albeit nervous, stock market situation encountered glum news indeed on their return to civilization." The members of the expedition were reunited with their planes, but many lost their fortunes.

The functional Fokker Universal was also the bush plane flown by Walter Edwin Gilbert, another Western Canada Airways (later to become Canadian Airways) pilot. Gilbert had enlisted in the RFC in the First World War and by 1918 was in France as a front-line fighter pilot. Back in Canada after the war, he flew forestry patrols and mapping missions across northern Manitoba and Saskatchewan. In 1929, when stationed in British Columbia, Gilbert had been instrumental in saving the life of H.C. Hughes, superintendent at the Emerald Mine in the West Kootenays. Hughes had been mauled by a grizzly bear and lost a lot of blood. Infection had set in, and he urgently needed to be flown out for treatment to save his life. Gilbert, under contract with the mine's owner, Consolidated Mining and Smelting Company, got the call. An experienced pilot was needed to pick up the patient and deliver him to a critical-care hospital as quickly as possible. Gilbert took on the mission. He flew 280 miles (450 kilometres) from Stewart to Burns Lake to pick up Hughes in a mere 2 hours and 10 minutes. The next morning, he ferried the wounded man and an attendant 520 miles (835 kilometres) to Vancouver via Quesnel and Bridge River. Hughes survived thanks to Gilbert's flying skill and stamina.

Bush pilot Walter Gilbert was made a fellow of the Royal Geographical Society in recognition of his contribution to mapping the Arctic. He is shown here at The Pas, Manitoba, in 1929.
LIBRARY AND ARCHIVES CANADA PA-102345

This was only the beginning of Gilbert's phenomenal bush-flying career. He was transferred by WCA to Fort McMurray, Alberta, accompanied by his wife Jeanne, who flew with him so often that she logged more miles than any other woman in Canada prior to the Second World War.

They first stayed at the Franklin Hotel, then bought a tiny "wooden shack" just behind it. First World War flying ace, bush pilot and explorer Punch Dickins, also flying with WCA, was already stationed there.

In July 1930, Gilbert, his engineer Stan Knight, pilot Buck Buchanan and Major Lauchie (L.T.) Burwash of the federal Department of the Interior left on a government-sponsored aerial exploratory trip with three objectives: find the remains of members of the ill-fated Franklin Expedition, who had departed England in 1845 and perished after abandoning their ships while searching for the Northwest Passage; take aerial photos of northern coastlines; and record magnetic properties near King William Island in an attempt to verify the location of the north magnetic pole. Gilbert flew up the Boothia Peninsula, his plane outfitted with an aerial camera and a portable radio, a new device that allowed him to communicate with headquarters back in the Mackenzie River District. Arriving in the settlement at Coppermine, Northwest Territories, he proceeded to methodically map a large part of the Arctic coastline and the area of the North Pole.

The other pilot on the expedition, Buck Buchanan, had come along to retrieve the WCA (now CA for Canadian Airways) plane left behind by the MacAlpine party the year before. Designated "SK," she had been sitting outside at Queen Maud Bay, entrusted to a group of Inuit camped nearby. With time to spare before the supply ship arrived with their gear for the Franklin search, Gilbert and Buchanan retraced the MacAlpine flight path; looking down, they saw the plane moored right where she had been left. They touched down and checked her out. Other than a few rusty cables, SK appeared airworthy. Pushing their luck some more, they topped up her oil and poured in some gas. The engine caught first time. It was getting dark, so they set up camp for the night. After tossing back food rations, Gilbert noticed some Inuit approaching the campfire. He invited them to join him and Buchanan, but they declined. One man held out a closed fist. When he opened it, Gilbert saw the key to the plane's cabin in his palm. MacAlpine had left it with him for safekeeping, and he was now returning it to the plane's rescuers. Gilbert was touched by the Inuits' honesty. When he and Buchanan had pried open the cabin door earlier, everything inside was as it had been left. Returning to Coppermine the next morning in separate planes, Buchanan refuelled and waved as he flew off in Fokker Universal G-CASK, leaving Gilbert, Knight and Burwash to start their hunt for Franklin.

The many 19th- and 20th-century searches for clues to Franklin's fate had expanded knowledge of the islands and waterways of the Arctic Archipelago, but many questions remained about the expedition's tragic end. The Inuit had brought some medals to show authorities, but this time Burwash also had a map from an anonymous old sailor that purported to shown the location of Franklin's grave on King William Island. The three men lifted off into a clear sky, but then smoke billowed out of the engine. They returned to the airstrip. The diagnosis was a blown piston, and the correct part could only be installed by CA in Winnipeg. He needed a replacement plane. Now his aircraft radio would not work. Gilbert remembered there was a radio on board the supply ship *Bay Chimo*, which was about to depart. He leaped on board just in time and made the call.

The next morning, Gilbert was rousted out of bed by the roar of an engine low overhead. Running outside, he came face to face with a laughing Buck Buchanan and SK, newly outfitted and with a full tank of gas. The threesome threw their gear into the refurbished Fokker and took off. With Coppermine behind them, they ran into a blizzard and were forced down at Bernard Harbour, southwest of Sutton Island, for seven days and nights. Burwash was convinced the mission was cursed. Overflying more of the Arctic coast, Gilbert continued aerial mapping until they landed at Cambridge Bay for supplies. From there, he proceeded to the rocky, icy-strewn coast of King William Island and put down on the southern tip. They refuelled from a cache that had been left for them and picked up Dick Finnie, another Department of the Interior employee, who was making a film about the North. As they flew on to Victory Point, the compass needle became erratic and began spinning in circles. Gilbert was well aware of the effect magnetism had on compasses and pointed at Knight, who began operating the aerial camera as rapidly as possible. Then he gave Gilbert a thumbs-up. They had just been the first to fly over and photograph the north magnetic pole.

Reaching Victory Point, they set down on an ice-free inlet and rushed ashore. Burwash and Finnie took off to search, while Gilbert and Knight made camp. The next morning, the four men gingerly picked their way over sharp rocks that cut into the soles of their boots. Then Burwash sighted something. It looked like an abandoned campsite. Scattered around were food tins, a bit of dark-blue cloth and some metal fragments but nothing else—certainly no bones. The camp had remained undiscovered until then, but the few artifacts Burwash collected yielded no clues to the eventual fate of the campers. The next day, Gilbert flew around the island, Knight photographed its coastline and they flew back to Coppermine in silence.

They had been gone for three weeks and now set out for Fort Smith and its radio link to the outside world. Gilbert was surprised to learn the press had speculated that they too had been stranded at the mercy of the elements or died in an Arctic crash. He immediately sent word to Jeanne that he was very much alive and flew on to meet her at Fort McMurray, where the aerial explorers were greeted as heroes.

A year after Gilbert's party failed to find any remains of Franklin's crew, William Gibson of the HBC searched the south coast of King William Island and discovered a number of skeletons and artifacts from the Franklin expedition. In 1981 and 1982, anthropologists from the University of Alberta discovered the scattered remains of seven unidentified Franklin expedition crew members on King William Island.

In recognition of his contribution to mapping the Arctic, Gilbert was made a fellow of the Royal Geographical Society in 1932. He was awarded the McKee Trophy in 1933, "in recognition of his exploratory flights throughout the North." Gilbert settled into the life of a bush pilot in Fort McMurray, taking prospectors and miners on charter flights across the North. With Punch Dickins, he completed the first commercial flight to Port Radium on Great Bear Lake in 1931, and that same year the Canadian Press paid him to fly a reporter to Aklavik for an interview with Charles Lindbergh, the first man to fly non-stop from New York to Paris, and his wife, Anne Morrow Lindbergh. The couple were flying across Canada on a trip to China and the Far East. The next morning, when Lindbergh had difficulty lifting off in his heavily fuelled plane, Gilbert pulled in front and took off so Lindbergh could ride his slipstream up off the water and into the air.

CHAPTER

5

The Flying Knight of the Northland

CLENNELL HAGGERSTON DICKINS could not remember when he was not called "Punch." Born in Portage la Prairie, Manitoba, he moved to Edmonton with his family when he was 10. His nickname was bestowed either when his brother, Francis, called him Punch for some unknown reason, or when his maternal Aunt Nell called him a fat little punch because his clothes kept riding up over his tummy. However he received it, the nickname stuck for life. As a bush pilot he acquired other monikers. Northern Natives called him Snow Eagle, northern whites called him White Eagle, the press dubbed him The Flying Knight of the Northland and the Inuit called him Tingmashuk (birdman), although they were often very skeptical of his airplane because "the wings don't flap."

After enlisting in the infantry in the First World War, Dickins spent a less-than-exciting year as company clerk, then transferred into the RFC, where he became a bomber pilot, shooting down seven enemy aircraft and becoming one of the few bomber pilots designated an ace (a pilot with five or more kills). He modestly attributed his success to teamwork with his skilled gunner, Second Lieutenant Jock Adam, and by 1918 they had flown 73 missions together. Dickins was awarded the Distinguished Flying Cross (DFC) at age 20 in 1919. After returning home, he briefly studied engineering at the University of Alberta, then earned commercial-pilot certification and joined the new RCAF from 1924 to 1927. Seeking to impress a girl named Connie whom he had met at university, Dickins flew his plane under Edmonton's High Level Bridge over the North Saskatchewan River. It was a dangerous stunt but dramatic enough to catch Connie's attention. They married in 1927 and remained a devoted couple for almost 70 years.

Assigned to report to the Edmonton Post Office on the use of aircraft to deliver letters and packages faster than by rail or truck, he left the military for civil aviation. He joined WCA and convinced them of the profitable future for airmail, proving it by flying the first prairie airmail circuit, which included Regina, Calgary, Edmonton, Saskatoon and Winnipeg. Like fellow bush pilots, Dickins was fascinated by the new frontier, the North. During his long career, he flew more than 1,000,000 miles (1,610,000 kilometres) across the uncharted Arctic using nothing more than dead reckoning and his handmade maps because weather reports, accurate compass readings and even prepared landing strips were unknown. As a bush pilot, Dickins was reported missing many times, but he always made it out and back home. His exploits became legendary. Dickins delivered the first airmail over the Northwest Territories; he was the first pilot to fly along the Arctic coastline, the first to fly the full 2,000-mile (3,220-kilometre) length of the Mackenzie River, doing so in two days, and the first to fly prospectors to Great Bear Lake when uranium deposits were found there.

Throughout his life, Dickins was lucky. He walked away from many crack-ups without a scratch, leaving his planes to be picked up at a later date. He once ditched on a northern Ontario lake when his engine quit. He camped out, rationing his food to stretch over one week. Although he had brought his rifle along and could supplement his rations with wild game, he had no idea where he was. On day three of his encampment, he heard the roar of a plane and threw some more twigs on the fire. The search plane had spotted his signal fire and flown over to investigate. Seeing Dickins's waving arms, the pilot dipped his wings up and down and then landed to pick him up and fly him out.

It could have been much worse if Dickins hadn't been

wearing his usual cold-weather flying suit, which was a fur parka made entirely out of rat pelts. (They were probably muskrat pelts, but people liked the rat story better.) It was a unique wardrobe choice but essential to surviving in a harsh environment. Dickins counted on it to keep him snug and warm in the worst weather. It again proved its worth when he was forced down by a blizzard shortly after takeoff and had to walk through hip-high snow back to base.

In 1928, the parka accompanied him on a contract job for Lieutenant Colonel C.D.H. MacAlpine of Dominion Explorers. The job involved checking out locations along Hudson Bay and then parts of the unmapped Northwest Territories. Richard Pearce, the editor of *Northern Miner*, came along to write about the trip. Fuel caches would be available, but there would be long unexplored stretches of the Barrens to cover. They flew out of Winnipeg to Port Churchill and looked down on a pod of whales cavorting in the water below. Refuelling at Baker Lake, they flew over trackless tundra with not even a caribou herd in sight. For hours, there were no identifiable markers, and Dickins began to question his navigation. Were they going in the correct direction? The horizon was an indistinct blur with sky and land indistinguishable. He checked his rudimentary instruments and his maps, such as they were. He checked his own internal compass and sense of direction honed over years of bush flying. Cabin conversation ceased. The engine droned on. Finally there was a reflection from something down below. It was Dubawnt Lake. They had made it over the worst part of the Barrens. Turning south, Dickins put down at the RCMP post at Stony Rapids, where they spent the night and refuelled after MacAlpine had a wee private chat with the reluctant commandant, who at first claimed there was no fuel available for the plane.

The next morning, gassed up, they set out again, but there were strong headwinds that ate up fuel at an alarming rate. Then the needle in the fuel gauge stabilized at quarter-full. Dickins was relieved, but not for long. When the engine started sputtering, he realized the needle was not registering accurately because it had frozen. The engine was dead, and they needed a place to land immediately. Down below was the Slave River. Dickins lined up with the ribbon of water, looking to see if there were any deadheads just under the surface, or any sandbars or animals crossing. It looked clear, but there would be no second chance. He had to get it right the first time. The three men chucked up their safety harness for maximum restraint and prepared to go in. Dickins chose his spot, an area without dark shadows that would indicate any obstacles. The Fokker floated down and landed like a leaf on the water. As the plane headed into shore, the men jumped out, sloshed through the cold water and tied the plane to some trees with rope from its cargo compartment.

Over a campfire, the men discussed their options. Nobody knew where they were, so rescue was unlikely. They could abandon the plane and trek 60 miles (97 kilometres) with few supplies through unmapped bush in what they believed was the direction of Fort Smith. Dickins suggested they get the axe out of the plane, cut down some trees, build a raft and float downriver, hopefully to civilization. It was agreed that a raft was their best chance of getting out safely. MacAlpine and Pearce went to check out possible logs for the raft, and Dickins went to get the axe. Standing on one of the plane's floats, he stopped to catch a sound that was not made by Mother Nature. It sounded like the putt-putt-putt of an engine, but his engine was very dead. Then he heard the blast of a whistle coming from the river. He grabbed his binoculars and scanned the water. It was surreal. Coming around the bend, belching black smoke and churning the water, was a real live steamboat.

Dickins jumped back on shore and tore through the underbrush, shouting and waving his arms. The boat kept moving. Racing over rocks into a clearing, he yelled even more, jumping up and down on top of a high boulder. The boat slowed, started a turn and gave a loud blast. Somebody on board waved back. As the steamboat pulled near shore, a man in a red-and-black-checked wool jacket leaned over the rail and shouted, "Are you guys in trouble?"

Not any more, thought Dickins, but he shouted back, "Do you have any airplane fuel on board?"

"Sure do," was the reply. "Got ten drums for some guy called Dickins who is supposed to fly up here next winter."

In 1929, one of the first airmail planes in the North is loaded with mailbags at Fort McMurray, Alberta, en route to Aklavik, Northwest Territories. GLENBOW ARCHIVES NA-463-49

"I'll take them. I'm Dickins," came the response.

MacAlpine was flabbergasted. Pearce was madly scribbling in his notebook. Prescient or not, management back at WCA had decided to set up fuel caches along the riverbank for future flights they had scheduled for Dickins. The fuel had arrived just in the nick of time. Gassed up and good to go within an hour, Dickins lifted off and dipped his wings to the steamboat below before heading to Fort Smith with two very relieved passengers.

In spite of demonstrations to the contrary, the federal government still did not believe a private company could deliver mail quickly and reliably. WCA wanted to prove them wrong. On January 23, 1929, with engineer Lew Parmenter and postal inspector T.J. O'Reilly, Dickins was airborne from Edmonton, en route between Fort McMurray and Aklavik, Northwest Territories, on the Arctic coast. The temperature was -50°F (-45°C). On approach over Great Slave Lake for a stopover at Fort Resolution, Dickins checked out the frozen surface, then dropped down to land. Even his sharp eyes had failed to see a snow-covered hummock. They slammed into it with gut-wrenching force amid shooting chunks of ice and the sound of tearing metal. The plane had barely lurched to a stop before Dickins was outside looking at the damage. The left undercarriage was torn and the aluminum propeller blades bent. They had no replacement parts. The closest telegraph office was at Fort Smith, six days' travel by dogsled. If parts were available, they could be flown in, otherwise the three men would be stuck at Fort Resolution until spring when parts could be shipped by boat from Edmonton. Or, they could try to fix it. To the ever-confident Dickins, that seemed their best option. They stabilized the plane with some gas canisters under the left side, rigged a crude teepee out of poles and hides to cover the engine and then bedded down. Dickins pulled his rat furs around himself and drifted off to sleep.

The next morning, they crafted a replacement strut out of some metal pipe from Fort Resolution's plumbing system, then set to work hammering out the propeller blades. The first one went well, but the next blade broke. Dickins cursed. After a sleepless night, he and Lew decided to give it one more try. Remembering he had a hacksaw in his tool kit, Dickins pulled it out and began filing down the broken blade of the propeller, then taking an equivalent amount off the good blade. Reshaping both blades and then repointing the tips with a file was a time-consuming job, but by afternoon it was finally done.

"Looks pretty good," said Lew. "Take her up and try them out."

"Tell Connie I love her," Dickins said as he hopped in and Lew spun the prop.

Dickins turned the plane into the wind, opened the throttles and released the brakes. The plane moved forward but more slowly than usual. Dickins knew he had less power from the shorter blades, but he had a lot of lake. Gaining momentum, he pulled back on the control stick, and the plane lifted off. He was airborne. The next week, all three men were back in Edmonton and the plane was being repaired. Six months later, Dickins landed in Aklavik with the mail.

In 1929, Dickins flew to Fort Good Hope on the Mackenzie River and picked up the first shipment of furs ever sent by air to traders in Winnipeg. In January 1930, the federal government finally awarded WCA a contract to establish Prairie Air Mail Service, and Dickins made the inaugural flight. In November of that year, Canadian Airways bought out WCA but kept the staff. Dickins became superintendent of the Mackenzie District, and then of the entire northern operations, overseeing 20 planes and 50 men. But when the stock market crashed in 1929, unemployment rose, factories closed, drought decimated prairie crops and the Great Depression hit. Suddenly, fast mail delivery was not a government priority, and the contract was cancelled. That did not ground Dickins. In 1935, he flew bureaucrats studying mining operations, investigating northern air routes and mapping the Yukon.

In 1936, Dickins conducted an air survey of northern Canada that covered 10,000 miles (16,100 kilometres). When the Second World War broke out, he again enlisted, this time as head of the RAF's Atlantic Ferry Command, delivering combat aircraft to Britain, and then as a proponent of the British Commonwealth Air Training Plan, which taught flying skills to thousands of Allied aircrews in Canada. In the early 1940s, the Canadian Pacific Railway Company had bought up bush airlines in quick order, ending with Canadian Airways in 1942, to form Canadian Pacific Airlines (rebranded CP Air in 1968). By 1945, Dickins was the company's vice-president. Given the genesis of the company, management was an amalgam of early bush aviators: president Grant McConachie, Punch Dickins and Calgary depot manager Wop May.

Dickins later joined de Havilland Canada Aircraft Ltd. as a consultant. In 1946, de Havilland was looking to the civilian market to replace dwindling military work and decided to develop a new all-purpose transport plane for extreme northern conditions. They did what Fairchild and Noorduyn had done before—they asked seasoned bush pilots for input on specifications. Dickins collected recommendations that included an all-metal airframe, locating the battery cover for easy removal and installing doors on both sides of the fuselage so pilots could pull up quickly to either side of a dock to unload freight or passengers. The doors needed to be wide enough so a 45-gallon (205-litre) drum of fuel could be easily rolled in. Ideally, the planes would have extra power and STOL performance in a design that could be easily fitted with wheels, skis or floats. When de Havilland engineers said this would result in poor cruise performance, one pilot replied, "You only have to be faster than a dog sled."

Dickins was instrumental in the design and launch of the Chipmunk (DHC-1) and Beaver (DHC-2) planes. The Beaver is a single-engine, propeller-driven, high-wing, all-metal aircraft, designed to be a reliable, all-purpose utility machine. It seats six people and is often described as a half-ton truck with wings. The Beaver spawned the Otter (DHC-3), Caribou (DHC-4), Buffalo (DHC-5), Twin Otter (DHC-6) and Dash 7 (DHC-7), all durable work planes used worldwide from jungles to glaciers. For his ongoing accomplishments, Dickins became the second recipient of the McKee Trophy in 1928 for his pioneering flight across the Barrens. He was named an Officer in the Order of the

British Empire in 1936, an Officer of the Order of Canada in 1968 and a member of Canada's Aviation Hall of Fame in 1974.

In a 1962 speech, Dickins described bush flying as "a pilot and mechanic, who are ready and willing to take any kind of a load to any destination, on or off the map, within the limits of their aircraft, and the financial resources of the customer." He flew until he was 78 years old and died in Toronto in 1995 at the age of 96. His ashes were scattered by his son John along the Mackenzie River from an aircraft flown by another remarkable bush pilot, Max Ward.

CHAPTER

6

May, Mercy and a Manhunt

WOP MAY AND PUNCH DICKINS both grew up in the city of Edmonton, attended the same school, played on the same hockey team and enlisted in the new RCAF. Although very different in physique and personality, they were still called the "twins of the air." Named for Canada's seventh prime minister, Sir Wilfrid Laurier, May got a name change early in life when his two-year-old cousin could not get her tongue around the moniker Wilfrid. The best she could do was Woppie, shortened to Wop. His family thought it was cute, and the nickname stuck. May worked in his father's service station and became a skilled mechanic, acquiring expertise that would be useful later in life.

In 1910, the first airplane landed in Edmonton, and May

was hooked. He enlisted five years later when he saw a newspaper photo of a First World War fighter plane in the skies over France. But instead of pilot instruction, he was trained as a machine gunner. He kept telling his superiors he wanted a transfer to the RFC, and in 1917, he got it. The first day of flight instruction consisted of taxiing along the runway. He was bored, but was finally allowed to take off with his instructor in the seat behind. May buzzed the airfield, did a figure eight and totally ignored orders to land. Back on the ground, he was confined to quarters. After training, he and other new pilots were sent to St. Omar base in Belgium. To celebrate their front-line posting, they went on a two-day pub crawl through local towns. May was ordered back to base, but because pilots were needed, in April 1921 he took off as the junior flyboy in a squadron of Sopwith Camels.

May was ordered to observe but not engage in any dogfights with German planes. He couldn't help himself. When a German Albatross peeled off, May followed, lost him in the clouds, then picked him up again and fired. He scored a direct hit and the Albatross went down in flames. But May had problems of his own. His guns had jammed, and he needed to get back to base quickly. That's when the Red Baron spotted him. Baron Manfred Albrecht von Richthofen in his red Fokker Dr.1 triplane had May in his sights. No matter what he did, May could not shake the Red Baron. But suddenly, in the valley of the Somme River, the Baron's Fokker triplane shuddered, then arced to the ground, bursting into flames on impact. May's commander, Captain Arthur "Roy" Brown, wrote in his report of the incident: "I went back again and dived on pure red triplane which was firing on Lt. May. I got a long burst into him and he went down vertical and was observed to crash by Lieutenant Mellersh and Lieutenant May." May would not become the Baron's 81st victim. He looked back to see Brown, who had come to his aid.

But was it Brown's guns or the guns of the Australians on the ground below that had shot down the Red Baron? Nobody was officially credited with the kill, and the debate continues. Like the assassination of President John F. Kennedy in 1963, the death of Manfred von Richthofen is surrounded by conflicting eyewitness accounts and a mountain of speculation. In 1925, a New York magazine called *The Progressive* published an article titled "Richthofen Was Murdered." It reported rumours circulating in Germany that Richthofen had landed unscathed and that Canadian soldiers had jumped from their trenches and killed him before he could climb out of his triplane. The hearsay may have begun when German pilots from the Baron's "circus" reported witnessing the triplane's relatively smooth crash landing. This sparked hopes the Baron had been captured alive and later speculation that he had been murdered.

May racked up 13 kills of his own before the war ended and received the Distinguished Flying Cross. After returning home to Canada, Wop May and his brother

Court opened May Airplanes Ltd., Alberta's first airline, barnstorming and delivering the *Edmonton Journal* newspaper to Wetaskiwin. In early 1921, a new opportunity arose in the oil industry. During the summer, oil companies could move men and equipment by boat, but winter transportation was a big problem. Imperial Oil decided that planes were the answer and hired May and First World War veteran pilot George Gorman to travel to New York and fly two new planes back to Edmonton. Mechanical problems and bad weather lengthened their return trip, but people followed their progress on radio news reports. Finally, on January 15, 1921, they landed in Edmonton and were greeted by thousands of people.

May wanted to continue the air-shipping business, but in 1924 he married Violet "Vi" Bode, a noted equestrienne, so needed to find a "real" job. He sold the flying business and joined National Cash Register (NCR), moving to Ohio. While there, he was struck in the eye with metal from a lathe, which seriously impaired his vision for the rest of his life. Convinced his future lay with flying, May returned to Edmonton and founded the Edmonton and Northern Alberta Aero Club in 1927, fulfilling the roles of president, chief pilot, mechanic and instructor.

On New Year's Day, 1929, M.R. Bow, deputy minister of health for Alberta, received a telegram from Dr. Harold Hamman of Fort Vermilion: "Diphtheria. Fear Epidemic, Send Antitoxin." The manager of the HBC post in Little Red

River and his wife had contracted the contagious disease, but Hamman had no antitoxin for them or any other victims. Hamman had raced by dogsled from Little Red River back to Fort Vermilion and convinced a resident with a sled and team of horses to take the news to the telegraph office in Peace River. The overland trip took 12 days. More than two weeks had passed since the telegram had been received, and it would take even longer to deliver serum back 600 miles (965 kilometres) north of Edmonton. By then everybody could be dead.

Bow telephoned Wop May, who immediately volunteered to fly the mercy mission, as did engineer Vic Horner. Their plane was a small Avro Avian, which had an open cockpit, no heater and no skis. They would be landing, or crashing, on wheels in snow. The serum would survive, or perish, with them, and if it froze, it would be useless. The 600,000 units of serum, enough for 200 people, were wrapped in blankets and placed in the freight compartment of the aircraft. May and Horner knew that the blankets could catch fire so close to the heat of the engine, but there was no other way. Just before takeoff, May's wife, Vi, rushed over with a handful of chocolate bars, just in case. They disappeared into -60°F (-51°C) temperatures that penetrated all their layers of clothing—wool, leather and fur—flying at 500 feet (152 metres) through blinding ice fog. Their goggles froze on the outside and misted on the inside. Sharp crystals cut their faces until they bled. After four hours, they flew out of the fog bank near McLennan Junction, south of Peace River, where a surprise greeted them.

They were looking at a makeshift airstrip, snow tamped down and flags lining the edge. Alerted by radio that May and Horner were coming, residents had prepared the runway and now stood beside it waving. As they climbed out of the plane, May and Horner were stiff from cold and immobility and thrilled at the offer of hot food and a warm bed for the night. They had come 267 miles (430 kilometres); they still had 320 miles (515 kilometres) more to go.

Setting off the next morning, May and Horner made Peace River by noon and refuelled. While stopped there, they tucked the serum inside their clothing next to their bodies because, just as they had feared, the blankets wrapped around the serum had caught fire, and they'd had to beat out the flames with their gloved hands. Aloft again and on the way to Fort Vermilion, they hit a blizzard. The little plane pitched and yawed as it was buffeted by strong winds and sleet that slashed their already cut faces. Luckily they were so cold they could not feel it. Through it all, May managed to keep his bearings, and by late afternoon they sighted their destination. Dr. Hamman and the settlers helped the men out of their plane because they were too cold and fatigued to move on their own. The doctor rushed off to Little Red River by dogsled. It was too late for the HBC manager and his wife, but the antitoxin delivered by May and Horner did save the rest of the community. On January 6, the pair landed back in Edmonton, where thousands of people watched the mayor award each of them a gold watch. May just wanted to get home and warm up.

The following year, May was offered a flying job with Commercial Airways Ltd. in 1930. He made the first non-stop flight between Edmonton and Winnipeg, and as a publicity stunt, raced a train to see who could deliver freight faster. May had completed the return trip before the train finished one leg of the journey, thus earning a contract to fly mail from Fort McMurray to northern communities. Aklavik now had delivery three times a year. He flew food to Peace River residents marooned by flood waters and oxygen canisters to a farmer with pneumonia. He was an angel of mercy and soon would also be a champion of justice.

In late 1931, a trapper came to the RCMP post in Aklavik to file a complaint that somebody was damaging his traps. He suspected a local weirdo named Albert Johnson, who had a cabin on Rat River near Fort McPherson, Northwest Territories. Constable Alfred King and Special Constable Joe Bernard set off by dogsled to investigate. Finding no one at the cabin to respond to their shouts and knocks, they returned 60 miles (97 kilometres) to Aklavik, got a warrant and went back to the cabin. This time they were met by gunfire. King was hit in the chest and fell. Bernard tied the bleeding officer to his dogsled and mushed back to Aklavik. Then he returned over the well-worn route with a posse of nine police officers, some trappers and a guide. They got the same reception—

even more rifle fire from inside the cabin. One officer crawled closer and tossed a stick of dynamite beside the outside wall. It exploded in a firestorm of flying wood chunks, snow and earth. But when he looked up to see how much of the cabin remained, he had to dive back down as more shots whizzed over his head. This was going to be tougher than originally thought. The posse went back to Aklavik and returned five days later with more supplies and reinforcements, only to find the cabin abandoned and footprints in the snow.

For the next 48 days, the RCMP chased their man, dubbed the Mad Trapper of Rat River by the media, into the Richardson Mountains. He went in circles and followed caribou herds to hide his trail, which meant the tracking dogs could not keep his scent. He didn't seem to have any supplies with him, yet he was not slackening his pace, even though temperatures hovered around -40°F/C. By the end of January, the Mounties were no closer to catching the fugitive. Then one day, with the crack of a rifle shot, Constable Edgar "Spike" Millen fell down dead. The Mad Trapper had graduated to murder.

Inspector A.N. Eames knew the RCMP needed help and appealed to Punch Dickins, now WCA superintendent for the Mackenzie District and based in Edmonton. Dickins offered the services of his chief pilot, Wop May, to provide aerial assistance and keep the team supplied. May flew north with mechanic Jack Bowen and Constable William Carter, who was replacing Constable Millen. In his Bellanca

CH-300 Pacemaker, May flew over every inch of Yukon forest looking for any anomaly, and airlifted patrols into the mountains to get ahead of Johnson and cut him off before he reached Alaska. Takeoff from makeshift airstrips was so difficult that May often had to tie the plane to a tree, rev the 220 kW (300-hp) engine to its maximum, then have one of the searchers chop the rope with an axe so he could slingshot himself into the air.

On February 17, May passed low over the Eagle River and noticed something below. It was the Mad Trapper dug into the snow. May directed the trackers to the spot and watched as they approached. One man fell as he was shot. The others closed in, and a volley of shots ended the life of Albert Johnson. May set his plane down and approached the bullet-riddled corpse, then moved over to Sergeant Earl Hersey, who had been shot. The men bundled him into the plane, and May flew at top speed to Aklavik for medical treatment, making the 125-mile (200-kilometre) journey in 45 minutes. He knew every pass and peak in the mountains, knowledge that proved invaluable when they ran into a blizzard on the way. Hersey survived, but the doctor said if they had been 15 minutes later, the sergeant would have died.

May had to return to pick up the trapper's frozen corpse and take it back too. Nobody knew anything about the man, and his final possessions were bizarre. Among them were 32 kidney pills, $2,410 in Canadian and American bills (worth approximately $60,000 today) and two glass jars containing five pearls and seven pieces of gold dental work. He had been packing a .22 Winchester rifle, a model 99 Savage, a .30-30 rifle and a large supply of ammunition. No motive for his crimes was ever established.

In 1932, Canadian country-music singer Wilf Carter immortalized the event when he recorded the song "The Capture of Albert Johnson" at RCA Victor in Montreal. But who was Albert Johnson? The initial 1930 investigation of his identity focused on an obscure individual named Arthur "Mickey" Nelson who trapped and prospected in the same west-central Yukon area and owned guns similar to Johnson's. In 2009, Discovery Channel televised the August 11, 2007, exhumation of Johnson's corpse. DNA samples were taken before the body was re-interred and compared with DNA from relatives of all potential Mad Trapper candidates. The test results excluded all of them with 100 percent probability. Analyses of isotopes in Johnson's teeth indicated he was not Canadian but likely grew up in the American Midwest or possibly Scandinavia. He was determined to be in his 30s at death.

After the chase, May returned to flying men and equipment into the North as resource companies raced to find oil and minerals. But the vision in May's eye, injured during his employment at NCR, was deteriorating, and the eye became so painful that he had it removed in 1937. That ended his flying career. With the start of the Second World War and the need for skilled pilots, May managed recruit training in

Heroic bush pilot Wilfrid Reid "Wop" May (left) and airplane mechanic Jack Bowen in the Northwest Territories in 1932.
GLENBOW ARCHIVES NA-1258-106

Edmonton as part of the British Commonwealth Air Training Plan and formulated techniques used by quick response aerial search-and-rescue teams at crash sites. The techniques worked so well that the US government awarded May the American Medal of Freedom in 1947. Like Oaks and Dickins, he received the McKee Trophy for establishing air services to remote regions and was inducted into Canada's Aviation Hall of Fame in 1974. May died of a heart attack while on a hiking trip in Utah in 1952.

CHAPTER

7

From Bush Life to Corporate Life

GEORGE WILLIAM "GRANT" MCCONACHIE was one of the few pilots to make a successful transition from domestic bush flying to the international corporate boardroom. McConachie was born in Hamilton, Ontario, and grew up in Edmonton. Hooked on flying from childhood, he read everything he could find about aircraft and hung out at the Edmonton airfield. Sometimes real-life heroes like bush pilots Punch Dickins and Wop May would give in to his pleas and take him up for a ride. He couldn't wait to take flying lessons and saved money for them by looking after aircraft on the field.

McConachie studied engineering at the University of Alberta and took flying lessons at the Edmonton and Northern Alberta Aero Club. A quick study, he soloed in a de Havilland Moth, a light plane designed for recreational use and civilian training, after only seven hours of cockpit instruction. The club grounded him twice for carrying passengers without a commercial licence. In one instance, he took off with the club president's plane for four days—without permission. It was rumoured that he had flown a miner to the US, but there were no records, nothing could be proved and McConachie had charm and the ability to say all the right things at the right time. He could sell a ketchup popsicle to a man wearing a white suit.

McConachie had big dreams, envisioning an over-the-pole route to Europe instead of the longer route across the Atlantic then in use. In 1931, with his commercial pilot's licence finally in his pocket, the 22-year-old McConachie looked for a flying job. As other pilots were finding out, during the Great Depression the Canadian government was not interested in airmail or air freight, and people could not afford to fly as paying passengers. So McConachie turned west, so far west that he planned to cross the Pacific Ocean to fly for Chinese National Airways. They were offering $300 a month, with the proviso their pilots had to serve in the military during times of war. After taking the train to Vancouver on the first leg of his journey to his new employer, McConachie dropped in to visit his father's brother. It was a serendipitous event that would change his life. Not wanting to risk his nephew's life in a country then at war with Japan, Uncle Harry proposed a business deal.

Harry would buy a plane and Grant would fly it. He bought a much-used old Fokker aircraft and told him to start his own airline. McConachie did just that. He chose Edmonton, the bush pilots' gateway to the North, as his base of operations. His first commission was flying fresh fish in Alberta from Cold Lake to Bonnyville. He took jobs other pilots wouldn't touch. He loaded in fresh fruit and vegetables and sold them from the plane, anything to make money. In a few months, he had repaid Uncle Harry and become a real bush pilot, flying trappers, surveyors, prospectors, huskies, oil barrels, meat and fish all over the North and barnstorming at fairs in the summer. Within a year, his company, Independent Airways, had three planes underwritten by Uncle Harry.

In November 1932, a trapper came to authorities in Edmonton with an urgent message. Two men had serious burns from a gas-pipe explosion at the telegraph station in Pelican Rapids and would not survive the trip out by dogsled. Getting them out by air would be a chancy proposition. The area was heavily forested, and the ice would still be too thin to support a plane. McConachie was the only pilot who thought it was a manageable risk. The military refused to send a doctor along but did throw in some medical supplies. McConachie sent a message back to have the men moved 10 miles (16 kilometres) to Oboe Lake, which had a beach where he could land, and to set a small bonfire there so he could judge wind speed and distance.

When McConachie and his mechanic Chris Green reached the pickup site, they saw a huge fire with smoke that obscured the view of the lake. Skimming in just above stall speed, McConachie looked for an area of beach wide enough to set down on; he then cut the engine. The plane dropped onto the sand, spewing up fine gravel and twigs. Then came a horrible tearing noise. The plane stopped when a tree root slashed right down its fabric fuselage. McConachie jumped out with the medical kit and ran over to where the two victims and some trappers had taken shelter from his violent landing. Two charred and oozing bodies were lying on makeshift litters. McConachie bandaged them while Green bandaged the plane. With the four men on board and ready to go, McConachie realized he didn't have enough room to take off. There were no brakes on the wheels to hold back the plane while he revved the engine, so he reverted to the old rope-around-a-tree technique. When the plane reached full power, he stuck his arm out and made a chopping motion. A trapper lifted his axe and chopped the rope. The plane shot forward and lifted off to fly to Edmonton.

There was no downtime for McConachie between assignments. Only a busy bush pilot made money. It was time to start flying fish again. Along with the colder weather came fog, and just as McConachie was about to take off early one morning he saw his Uncle Harry coming out of the mist. While on the train from Toronto to Vancouver, he had impulsively got off to see his nephew. They chatted for

In the mid-1930s, Natives help bush pilot Grant McConachie (fourth from left) make emergency repairs to an undercarriage strut of his fish-hauling bush plane. LIBRARY AND ARCHIVES CANADA C-061897

some time as tiny water droplets built up on the propeller blades and turned to ice. McConachie didn't notice the problem until he was halfway down the runway. He knew he didn't have enough speed to take off, but he had no room to stop either. Slowly the plane lifted off the ground, but it had no power to climb. McConachie just missed the smokestack near the CN railyards, then electric power lines appeared directly in his path. He turned sharply, but one wing clipped the ground and the plane cartwheeled end over end. Rolling into a ball to protect his head, he waited for the gas tanks to explode, wondering if he would look like those burned men he had evacuated from Oboe Lake. The plane stopped rolling in a field. All was silent. Then he heard the noise of people and vehicles. As McConachie moved to get a better look, the pain was instantaneous. Small wonder—his legs were bent at unnatural angles, it hurt to breathe and metal was sticking out of his thigh. First responders gave him whisky, and by the time he was pulled free of the wreckage the pain had lessened. In hospital, the X-rays showed 17 leg fractures, broken hips, plus shattered fingers, ribs and left kneecap.

After two months of recuperation, McConachie still limped badly. The reconstructed knee would not bend. He decided to be his own doctor and asked some barroom buddies to bend it for him as he placed it over the edge of a table. It hurt like hell and swelled up like a balloon, but now he could move it a bit. Months later, the knee buckled as he lifted fuel drums out of his plane, but after the pain subsided he had almost full flexibility. He would need it on his next assignment, when he flew a team of prospectors to an abandoned gold mine in the Stikine Range. Dodging sharp peaks and landing in deep snow on Two Brothers Lake, he and his passengers had to tramp the snow down with their snowshoes to make a runway so McConachie could take off to fly back to Edmonton.

On the airfield in Edmonton, McConachie was hit with

a bombshell. Uncle Harry and his business partners were in trouble; in fact, they were bankrupt. McConachie's planes were slapped with liens, and Independent Airways was grounded. McConachie managed to smooth-talk the creditors into releasing one plane so he could barnstorm to pay off the debt. The plane crashed. The cardinal rule of bush flying is that you always pick up everyone you dropped off, but McConachie now had no way to pick up the prospectors at Two Brothers Lake. After six frantic weeks trying to beg, borrow and do anything short of stealing a plane, he was able to fly in with a mining company team and pick up the emaciated prospectors, who could barely stand. When he went to the hospital to talk with team leader Barney Phillips, instead of a reprimand, McConachie got a job offer. Phillips was starting his own bush operation, United Air Transport (UAT), to serve his miners in the West and take on other jobs as available. Would McConachie fly for him? The answer was yes. Based out of Calgary, UAT hauled over one million pounds (453,600 kilograms) of fish from 1934 to 1935.

In 1935, oil executive Bob Wilkinson wanted to be flown from Calgary to Vancouver, and McConachie agreed to take him on the first commercial flight across the Canadian Rockies. The press followed their progress, and they were met by the mayor of Vancouver, who thought this was the start of a regular commercial air route. When he found out it was not, he refused to cover McConachie's bill at the

Hotel Vancouver. Since there was no agreement in writing about who would pay for accommodation, McConachie had to barnstorm the entire summer to pay it off, joining the prairie circuit of Ringling Brothers Circus and offering passenger rides for a-penny-a-pound of body weight. He stopped only long enough to marry Margaret MacLean, a nurse he had met while recuperating in 1932.

As the national economy improved and interest in fast mail delivery revived, UAT landed airmail contracts between Fort St. John and Fort Nelson, Edmonton, Whitehorse, Vancouver and Prince George, but with 12 planes on floats or skis, they still could not turn a profit. They needed larger, wheeled aircraft and prepared runways. The company bought three Fleet Freighter aircraft, and in 1939, it became Yukon Southern Air Transport.

At the beginning of the Second World War, business was slow and pilots were scarce. The federal government had decided in 1937 that it needed a nationwide air carrier. Fearful that the two US airlines would expand into Canada, it formed Trans-Canada Airlines (TCA). There were private interests that wanted their own national airline, too. Canadian Pacific Railway (CPR) began buying up small bush-flying companies, including Yukon Southern in 1941, and started Canadian Pacific Airlines (CPA) with McConachie as one of their executives. When the war in the Pacific and the threat of a Japanese attack on North America raised concerns about moving men and machinery on the West Coast, McConachie did aerial surveillance for the CANOL project and the 1,600-mile (2,575-kilometre) Alaska Highway from Dawson Creek, Yukon, to Fairbanks, Alaska. The highway was completed in 1943.

McConachie received the McKee Trophy in 1945 for his pioneering efforts in forging air service to the North. He became president of CPA in 1947. His fleet of DC-8s fulfilled his dream of a polar route, and he inaugurated CPA passenger service to Australia, Japan and Hong Kong, adding another 15,535 miles (25,000 kilometres) of flight routes by 1957 and flying worldwide negotiating new deals.

McConachie died of a heart attack in 1965. In 1968, his wife and two sons were present for the opening of Grant McConachie Way, an expressway leading to Vancouver International Airport.

In pioneer bush flying, Edmonton was referred to as the Gateway to the North. Edmonton companies built and repaired the planes and boats used by adventurers to discover and extract northern riches—fish, furs, gold, silver, radium or diamonds—and fly them to southern markets. Maxwell "Max" William Ward was born in Edmonton, where bush planes were a familiar sight in the skies and on the ground at the municipal airport. He was inspired by famous Edmonton bush pilots like Dickins and May, and wrote, "My whole idea of adventure, of living, was tied up in the notion of joining their ranks some day in a magnificent flying machine." As a child, Ward spent a lot of time walking around the fabric-covered wooden craft. He carved planes from pieces of wood at home and ran down the street holding then aloft and making "vroom" sounds like a zooming plane.

After a short stint at Canadian National Railways, Ward joined the RCAF, receiving his wings at age 20 in 1941. He was promptly assigned to the British Commonwealth Air Training Plan as an instructor. He wasn't good at following instructions himself, often flying lower than assigned and flying off to meet his sweetheart, Marjorie, in Calgary.

Following the war, Ward went to Yellowknife and bought a small de Havilland Tiger Moth biplane to fly passengers and freight as Polaris Charter Company Ltd. But the plane was small and had a limited range, needing to be refuelled every 130 miles (210 kilometres). On one trip to Edmonton, he had to land on a baseball diamond in Athabasca, interrupting the game in progress. Pulling out a 10-gallon (45-litre) drum he carried with him in the cockpit, he proceeded to refuel his plane, taxi and lift off, waving to the surprised players as he flew away. Ward next purchased a de Havilland Fox Moth. It held three passengers and up to 500 pounds (227 kilograms) of cargo and would be a step up for his business. He took the train to Toronto to pick it up. Flying back from Toronto, he landed at Kenora, Ontario, for the night. It wasn't until he hit the pile of gravel on the airstrip that he knew he should have looked more closely. The runway was being graded and the work crew had

Max Ward pilots his small CF-DJC de Havilland Fox Moth at Snare River, 90 miles (145 kilometres) west of Yellowknife, in 1947.
LIBRARY AND ARCHIVES CANADA PA-089954

left a pile just where he came in. Ward walked away with cuts and bruises, but his smashed-up plane took five weeks to repair.

Ward's next adventure occurred when his engine quit while he was flying into Arsenault Lake. After making a perfect landing, he found the problem: there was no oil. Somehow the oil-pan drain valve had opened, and he had been leaking oil throughout the trip. Now the Fox Moth needed a new engine. Ward hiked to a nearby drilling camp, hitched a ride back to Yellowknife, ordered a new engine from de Havilland on credit, went to Edmonton by train to take delivery, hitched a ride back to the drilling camp with another pilot and then walked four miles to and from the lake every day while he installed the new engine. Then he flew back to Yellowknife and another nasty encounter. Unable to show Air Transport Board bureaucrats that he had the required commercial flying licence on his own, he acquired a partner who did have such a commodity, and they established Yellowknife Airways Ltd.

Ward left the company in 1949 over operating differences and moved his family from Yellowknife to Lethbridge, where he earned a living as a construction worker with Marjorie's father and flew for Associated Airways just to keep his skills sharp. In 1951, after just six months with the company, he crashed while taking an HBC manager to Bathurst Inlet in the high Arctic. His departure had been delayed, his compass was useless so close to the north magnetic pole, and the sun was setting faster than his plane could fly, so navigating by sight was impossible. Then the fog came in. Ward knew he had to get down and tried to see a suitable spot. What looked like a lake turned out to be a high hill. He slammed the skis into it and ricocheted down the other side. He radioed for rescue, then waited five days for help to arrive. The first rescue plane got lost and had to refuel, but finally an RCMP plane spotted them and radioed in their position.

Ward finally got his own Class 4B Charter licence to operate a commercial air service. He bought the first de Havilland Otter used in Western Canada for $100,000, twice the cost of the average bush plane of the day, but the

Otter was bigger and faster and had a range of 600 miles (965 kilometres), three times that of his little Fox Moth. The plane credited with developing the North, the Otter could handle an impressive payload while gliding onto and off lakes. With the same overall configuration as the Beaver, but longer and heavier, with a wider wingspan and capable of seating up to 11 people, the Otter easily landed entire sheets of plywood and 16-foot (5-metre) lengths of lumber. One builder noted that you could tell which cabins had been built after the Otter was in service because their roofing consisted of whole sheets of plywood instead of sawn lengths that had to be pieced together. More planes, more work and more money followed.

By May 1953, Wardair Ltd. was in business, first operating domestically and then expanding into overseas charters. The airline had some unique assignments in the early years. On one occasion, a Texas rancher wanted a musk ox to crossbreed with his cattle, so two Wardair planes located a herd on the tundra and separated a young specimen from the rest. After one plane landed, its flying cowboys roped the wild creature, tied its legs and stowed it in the cargo area. They neglected to sedate it. For Ward, who still pitched in to clean and maintain his planes, this was the ultimate messy job.

Ward took his company public in 1961 but retained controlling interest. By the mid-1970s, Wardair was Canada's third-largest commercial airline and largest international air charter carrier, but the company faced tough competition from Air Canada and CP Air as well as difficulties with government regulators. In 1989, Ward surprised Bay Street by selling his airline. It was yet another step in the familiar process of growing an airline by buying out the competition. In 1987, Pacific Western Airlines Corporation had purchased CP Air, which had already acquired Nordair and Eastern Provincial Airways. These four airlines were combined into Canadian Airlines International, which was further expanded with the purchase of Wardair but eventually taken over by Air Canada in 2000.

Having received many aviation and business awards, Ward was inducted into Canada's Aviation Hall of Fame in 1974. At the time, it was noted that "his lengthy and continuing efforts to responsibly service this nation's most northern frontier by air, despite adversity, together with his development of a viable international charter service, have been of outstanding benefit to Canadian aviation." The following year he was made an Officer of the Order of Canada.

As Max Ward discovered, flying in the North was a dangerous proposition, and it remains so today. In wild, unforgiving country, bush pilots are at the mercy of unforeseen circumstances. They live or die by their endurance and skill. But thanks to his skill and determination, Ward's one-man shoestring operation in the North grew into a multi-million-dollar charter operation that circled the globe.

CHAPTER

8

Tales from Mountain Valleys

WHILE THE ENGINEER DID MOST of the drudge work to keep bush planes flying, it was usually the pilot who scooped up most of the glory. When their names and exploits appeared in newspapers, the recognition got them more flying contracts. Francis Russell "Russ" Baker used the press with great success, growing a single-plane operation into Central BC Airways. Stories about his derring-do and pioneering flights into unexplored territory appeared regularly in BC papers. Baker flew through difficult mountainous terrain with prospectors and also conducted mercy flights, arriving just in time to rescue lost trekkers. Forestry wardens were flown on patrols over hundreds of miles to otherwise inaccessible areas by "veteran bush pilot Russ Baker."

Baker's reputation also brought him work from the Americans during the Second World War. Shortly after the US entered the war, following the December 7, 1941, Japanese attack on Pearl Harbor, came the military initiative to build a highway from western Canada to Alaska so Allied troops could be rapidly deployed north if the Japanese invaded North America. Baker was one of several bush pilots contracted to fly surveyors along the proposed route. He did that and a lot more. On January 5, 1942, 14 new Martin B-26 Marauder bombers left Gowen Field at Boise, Idaho, headed for the Aleutian Islands in Alaska. They were being flown by new members of the 77th Bombardment Squadron, 42nd Bombardment Group, Air Force Combat Command, many of whom had minimal training. On January 16, facing the probability of foul weather, they took off along a 1,000-mile (1,610-kilometre) route to Whitehorse, Yukon. They were equipped with pencil sketches rather than maps and had no electronic navigation aids.

By 6:00 PM, three of the B-26s were lost, running out of fuel and flying at low altitude because of snow squalls. The crews decided to crash-land at a suitable location, should they be lucky enough to find one. When a fairly wide valley with a flat floor was sighted amid the mountains, they decided to go for it. Two planes landed without incident by keeping their wheels up, which allowed the aircraft's fuselage to skim over the snow like a boat's hull. The third plane dropped its landing gear as a braking manoeuvre to lose speed and nosed over into four to five feet (1.2 to 1.5 metres) of snow. Fortunately, the pilot and co-pilot received only minor injuries, and the rest of the crew was unhurt.

The aircraft were all equipped with survival equipment, so the crews set up camp in the valley. At first light on January 17, a search was begun for the missing planes but was not successful. On January 18, they were spotted by some Curtiss P-40E fighter planes also en route to Alaska. Then "veteran bush pilot Russ Baker" was dispatched to rescue them. He arrived the next morning in a small Fokker equipped with skis and began airlifting the men to Watson Lake, Yukon. It took almost a week for Baker to ferry all 24 crewmen to safety. A few months later, salvage crews were sent to the wreck site to strip the planes of all useable parts, which were then airlifted out. The remaining skeletal frames were abandoned. The valley began to be called Million Dollar Valley, an exaggeration of the cost of the three B-26 bombers.

For his role in rescuing the air crews, Russ Baker was awarded the United States Air Medal for "exceptional daring and pilotage ability" in January 1942 by President Harry Truman. By the 1960s, only a few of the 5,266 B-26 Marauders manufactured had survived the war or the scrapyard, and aircraft enthusiasts began searching around the world for restorable aircraft. In 1971, the Million Dollar Valley wrecks were rediscovered, and everything that remained was retrieved. By 2006, one of them had been restored to flying condition and another was undergoing restoration.

Baker worked for his old friend Grant McConachie of CPA as a pilot delivering mail to the North. He was made senior captain and later divisional superintendent for CPA at Whitehorse. It was during his time at CPA that Baker realized there was great business potential for charter aircraft companies. In 1946, he left to co-found Central BC Airways, based in Fort St. James, with fellow pioneer pilot Walter Gilbert. Its mission was to provide reliable air service to those working in mining, forestry, trapping and hunting in western and northern mountain communities where access was constrained by weather, topography and marginal profitability. It was an iffy business proposition, but Baker made it work and bought out Gilbert's share in the business.

Baker started with two Beechcraft seaplanes, two employees and a contract with the BC Forest Service. To meet the expanding needs of the Forest Service, he acquired four more aircraft in 1947, and in 1948 became the proud owner of the first Beaver aircraft manufactured by de Havilland.

In 1947, Russ Baker became the first pilot to set down in the ancient land of the Naha, a wild and rugged area with no roads in and no roads out. Just a bit north of the 60th parallel in Canada's Northwest Territories, the Nahanni area includes one of the deepest canyon systems in the world and the turbulent Nahanni River, which cuts through the remote Mackenzie Mountains. Today Nahanni National Park Reserve is one of Canada's greatest treasures and a UNESCO World Heritage Site. But it once had a more mysterious and sinister reputation. In autumn 1946, the Canadian media began running stories about lost miners and hidden riches in a far northwest "tropical valley" in the Nahanni. These fanciful tales were a welcome break from post-war recovery news. A young cub reporter for the *Vancouver Sun*, Pierre Berton, who wrote many of the Nahanni stories, decided to race against his journalistic competition to be first on scene in the legendary Headless Valley of the South Nahanni.

The most common explanation of the origin of the valley's name dates from 1906, when prospecting brothers Willie and Frank McLeod attempted to take the Nahanni as an alternative route to Klondike gold. Rumours circulated that they had found the mother lode before misfortune struck. Their headless skeletons were discovered in 1908 by other prospectors. There were suggestions that Albert Johnson, the Mad Trapper, might have been involved in the deaths when he first came from the east to Yukon's Ross River area, but nobody knows for sure.

Encouraged by his editor, Hal Straight, Berton approached Russ Baker. Although no plane had ever landed in the remote Nahanni in winter, Baker was eager to try. In January 1947, Baker, Berton and *Vancouver Sun* photographer Art Jones flew north to Prince George on a commercial flight, where they were met by Ed Hanratty, Baker's mechanic, with a Junkers monoplane.

During that harsh winter, -60°F (-51°C) temperatures were recorded on a regular basis. Berton had been born in

Members of the Headless Valley Expedition, photographed in January 1947: (from left to right) Pierre Berton, Russ Baker and Art Jones. LIBRARY AND ARCHIVES CANADA PA-102384

the North and knew harsh winters. Baker also had many wintry bush escapades, once responding to a rescue plea for a ski-equipped plane to fly out 60 starving members of a road crew stranded in the snow 140 miles (225 kilometres) north of Fort St. James. Because the local lakes were still open, Baker had flooded a sandbar, which froze just enough for him to take off, his plane stripped down to lighten the load. He made the round trip 10 times from his makeshift runway, saving all the men. Berton wrote of Baker's prowess and his mercy flights: "Maimed loggers, dying Indians, expectant mothers, flu-ridden children, fever-stricken prospectors have all buffeted northern gales to safety in his planes."

The four men flew north in 100-mile (160-kilometre) segments, landing to repair a cracked cylinder, then to fly a pregnant woman to the closest hospital. At each stop, Berton radioed back a dispatch to his editor; these were syndicated across Canada and around the world. By February 1947, as they approached the Shangri-La, some 100 newspapers were following the adventure. At Fort Liard, they picked up an additional man, RCMP constable Jim Reid, who would serve as an unimpeachable witness. They headed on to Nahanni Butte, where they were greeted by Gus and Mary Kraus. The front pages of the February 16, 1947, newspapers declared:

> Headless Valley, NWT (delayed - INS)—We landed today bang in the center of "Headless Valley," the much talked about, much disputed core of the wild Nahanni country—our plane bounced on the rough ice like a prewar golf ball. It is the first time that a plane on skis has landed in this mysterious valley of the north.

As their Junkers' engine idled on the frozen river, the men quickly ran out and set up prepared road signs, took photographs and entered a small cabin where a surprise awaited them, according to a story that appeared in the *Vancouver Sun* on February 17:

> In the heart of this weird valley, deep in the grim sawtooth Nahanni Mountains where men have died for their gold, we found, of all things, a pin-up girl. Are you listening,

Rita Hayworth? More important, is your press agent listening?

Miss Hayworth, let us be the first to tell you that you are the official queen of Headless Valley. For it was your pretty head and scantily-clad torso that we found staring right at us out of a tattered and crumbling cabin in the forbidden valley.

Who placed you here in this empty, forgotten log shack in this dead and silent banshee wind we have no way of knowing, but very nice you looked smiling at us from a sun-soaked California beach as you adjusted the zipper on your white-necked bathing suit. Believe us, Miss Hayworth, you brought the only breath of the tropics that has ever kissed the snow-locked wastelands that stretches across the 10 miles of this valley of dead men.

Over Officer Reid's objections, Berton removed the photograph "for historic value," suggesting he would send it to Miss Hayworth for her autograph. Then they took off and flew farther upriver to Pulpit Rock, the Gate of the Nahanni River, before heading out of the area. Back in Vancouver, the newspaper declared the Headless Valley series the greatest newspaper adventure story since the war.

After his adventure with Pierre Berton, Russ Baker continued to build his business. The real success of Central BC Airways began in 1949 when Baker amalgamated struggling companies that included Kamloops Air Service, Skeena Air Transport, Associated Air Taxi, Whitehorse Flying Services, Queen Charlotte Airlines, Associated Airways,

Aero Engineering Ltd. and Airmotive Accessories Ltd. These acquisitions made Central BC Airways the third-largest airline in Canada at the time, after the larger Trans-Canada Airlines (later Air Canada), and Canadian Pacific Airlines.

Another opportunity came in 1951 when Central BC Airways won the contract to provide air support to the Aluminium Company of Canada (Alcan), which was building large smelters at Kitimat and Kemano. With more expansion in mind, Baker changed the name of Central BC Airways to Pacific Western Airlines in 1953 and began scheduled service between Vancouver and Kitimat. He was on his way from bush pilot to aviation executive. In 1957, Baker took over Canadian Pacific Airlines in Alberta and Saskatchewan. Prior to his untimely death from a heart attack in 1958 at age 48, he had laid the groundwork for air service between Calgary and Edmonton, as well as daily service from these centres to the Arctic Ocean coastline and beyond. He was buried in a high hilltop overlooking the lakes of Stuart, BC, his grave marked by an anodized Beaver aircraft propeller on the headstone.

In 1975, Baker was inducted into Canada's Aviation Hall of Fame for "his unflagging efforts to provide safe, reliable, all-weather air service to the residents of Canada's western reaches and northern frontier." Today, aviation history buffs visit the Russ Baker Memorial, a one-third–scale model of the German Junkers W34 floatplane, known as the workhorse of the North, erected at Cottonwood Park in Fort St. James.

CHAPTER

9

Women Take to the Skies

MANY MILITARY PILOTS WHO SAW action during the First World War returned to Canada and took up barnstorming to earn a living before becoming bush pilots. But it wasn't only male pilots who performed aerial acrobatics and barnstormed across open skies. Pioneering female pilots also proved their flying abilities to amazed onlookers; however, several decades would pass before women would fly paying passengers into the Canadian wilderness.

Eileen Vollick, Canada's first licensed woman pilot, knew by age 19 that she wanted to fly. It was 1927, and Charles Lindbergh had just flown non-stop across the Atlantic, while Amelia Earhart was capturing public attention. Vollick had already parachuted into Burlington Bay near Hamilton, Ontario, in the summer before she started lessons at the flying school owned by Jack V. Elliot at Ghent's Crossing. Len Tripp, Vollick's instructor, had only one reservation about her: at five foot one, she had to sit on a pile of pillows to see out the cockpit of the ski-equipped Curtiss JN-4 Canuck biplane (known as a "Jenny"), registration G-CANY. She demonstrated takeoffs and landings on the frozen bay, performed five figure eights and flew 175 miles (282 kilometres) cross-country navigating by sight and landing perfectly. The comptroller of civil aviation issued Vollick private pilot's licence number 77 on March 13, 1928.

Vollick flew in the US and Canada, barnstorming and performing aerobatic rolling and spinning manoeuvres. Aerobatic flying requires a broader set of piloting skills and exposes the aircraft to greater structural stress than normal flight, but Vollick loved it. But in 1929 she met and married James Hopkin and moved to New York City, far away from stunt or bush flying. There they raised two daughters. Vollick died in 1968. In 1976, the Ninety-Nines, an international organization of female pilots, and the Ontario Heritage Foundation unveiled a plaque honouring her historic achievement; it is located in front of the Canadian Warplane Heritage Museum at the airport in Hamilton, Ontario.

Another woman with an early passion to fly was Vi Milstead. Born in Toronto in 1919, Milstead was the daughter of a carpenter. Money was scarce in the Great Depression, but she worked double shifts in a wool shop to earn extra money for pilot training. She learned to fly at the old Barker Field in Toronto, named in honour of Lieutenant Colonel W.G. "Bill" Barker, Canada's most decorated First World War pilot. Milstead passed her private pilot's flight test in 1939, got her commercial licence in 1940 and earned her instructor's rating in 1941. She was an instructor until civilian flying was halted in Canada because of gas rationing in 1942.

In 1943, at the age of 24, Vi Milstead joined the British Air Transport Auxiliary (ATA) and flew new fighter planes from factories to military bases across England and Allied Europe. She had approximately 1,000 flying hours and easily passed her check-out in a Harvard AT-6. Milstead piloted 27 different types of single-engine aircraft and 17 different types of advanced twin-engine aircraft as a first officer (equivalent to the military rank of captain). She was the longest serving Canadian female pilot in the ATA. Her favourite aircraft were the Spitfire and the de Havilland Mosquito. At war's end, she resumed her career as a flight instructor and pilot and went on to become one of Canada's first female bush pilots.

Milstead married Arnold Warren in 1947, and they moved to Sudbury, in northern Ontario, to fly for Nickel Belt Airways. Her work included flying surveyors to inspect mining sites, trappers returning back to their cabins with supplies, and sports hunters and fishers. Another task was spotting and reporting forest fires, and she also flew in men who had been recruited in local beer parlours to fight these fires. They were not always in the finest condition, and she had to encourage the odd one to leave the comfort of the aircraft and get on with firefighting. Flying a Fairchild Husky, Milstead also taught pilots how to land and take off on floats during summer and skis in winter. After two years on assignment in Indonesia with a United Nations organization, Vi and Arnold returned to Canada, where Milstead followed her interest in recreational aviation. She was inducted into Canada's Aviation Hall of Fame in 2010.

Like Vi Milstead, Moretta Fenton Beall "Molly" Reilly worked to support the war effort. When the Women's Division was formed in 1941, Reilly was one of the first recruits and became an aerial photographer. Reilly had really wanted to fly with the RCAF in the Second World War, but at that time women were not permitted to be military pilots. She served in Canada as a non-commissioned officer until 1946. Post-war, Reilly earned her pilot's licence and got a job with Southern Provincial Airlines in Ontario, flying Douglas DC-3s and Twin Beech aircraft. In this position she participated in the development of the airline's air-ambulance service throughout eastern Canada.

In the late 1950s, Reilly was promoted to captain, the first woman in Canada to carry this title. In 1959, she was hired as co-captain of a DC-3 by Peter Bawden Drilling

Services in Calgary to fly to major oil fields in western and northern Canada, including Frobisher Bay and Resolute Bay in the Arctic. She became the first to pilot the DC-3 during long periods of darkness and extreme weather, often without radio communication and navigation aids. In 1965, Reilly moved to Edmonton to join Canadian Coachways (later known as Canadian Utilities) as the company's chief pilot. She had modifications made to her Beechcraft Duke twin-engine plane to improve its performance in severe northern conditions. When Reilly finally retired, she'd flown more than 10,000 hours as corporate pilot-in-command, all without a single crash. She was inducted into Canada's Aviation Hall of Fame in 1974 for "her dedication to flight" and "her self-set demands for perfection."

Dedication came naturally to Ruth Parsons. She was born into a family of bush pilots in 1933. Her four older brothers flew fish, furs, trappers and miners along with their equipment around northern Ontario. Parsons earned her private pilot's licence in 1952 and her commercial licence in 1954, working part-time at the public library for 50 cents an hour to pay for lessons. As a fallback plan, she enrolled in teachers' college, earned her certification and taught in Fort William for three years.

When Parsons went to Kenora for float certification, her brother Keith, who was aboard as a passenger, decided to test her skills on the way. His theory was that any pilot who could fly a plane while scared stiff was competent to be in the air. Parsons was not aware of this peculiar instructional technique. As she was lining up to land, he threw his arms up in front of his face and screamed, "What are you doing? Look out, you're going to kill us!" Ignoring the outburst, she landed safely and taxied over to the dock. Getting out, Keith grinned at her and said, "You'll do fine, kid." She did—but she never flew with him again.

In 1955, Parsons began flying full-time, bringing tourists into Gold Point Farm Camp, which was built near an old mine claim on Shoal Lake. The camp was owned by Barbara Machin, whose parents had emigrated from England, bringing elegant furniture from their grand English home to the northern woods. The furniture now graced the main lodge. Parsons stayed there from breakup to freeze-up while flying in guests and supplies in Machin's Stinson 108. In winter, she returned to an apartment in Kenora, switched Machin's plane from floats to skis and flew charters for her brothers' Parsons Airways Northern.

Seeking a good trout-fishing area, Machin decided to build a second camp at isolated Carroll Lake, near the Manitoba border. Parsons had to fly in everything—building supplies, workmen, food, fuel and, later, guests. A local trapper was not pleased about the new neighbours. After a boat and some gas drums disappeared from the camp, Parsons spotted the boat from the air. There were holes chopped in its bottom, and it had been filled with rocks and abandoned near some rapids in the river. There was no proof the trapper had done it, but who else could it have been?

One day after the camp opened, Parsons arrived to find the trapper in the kitchen spinning bizarre tales about his shooting prowess to the guests. He had been on his own too long and was obviously "bushed." He believed the lake was his and talked to the water.

"Would you shoot me?" Parsons asked him.

"Only if I had to," came the reply. Yet when Parsons was getting married, the trapper gave her a wedding present, a fully equipped tackle box. He left it at the camp along with a note saying he had a pressure cooker that he had been using as a still, but if she wanted it he would give it to her. Parsons declined his offer. He drowned shortly afterward, possibly after consuming too much of his moonshine.

On what should have been an ordinary milk run to the new camp, Parsons loaded the Stinson (which she called her "station wagon") and boarded her passengers, who were workmen finishing some trim work at the lodge. It was a perfect flying day as she took off, climbed and cruised at 3,000 feet (914 metres), enjoying the view and marvelling that she got paid to do this. When a passenger started yelling, memories of her brother returned. But this was a real emergency. Smoke was coming from her seat and flames were visible. Parsons put down on a lake in record time as her passengers calmly smothered the fire. It turned out that the plane's battery had been moved in a modification to the aircraft, but because the cover hadn't been replaced, the battery had shorted and ignited her seat. Parsons had that oversight corrected immediately.

In 1958, Parsons married Ontario Provincial Police officer Larry Moore and moved to Red Lake, where she did some instructing before returning to teaching. Although Parsons, her husband and three children flew in their Cessna 180, her bush-flying days were over.

Today, women are not only bush pilots, they also fly and repair large commercial and military aircraft and helicopters, navigate hot-air balloons and fly into space. The Ninety-Nines Inc., the world's oldest and largest organization of licensed women pilots, was founded on November 2, 1929, by 99 female pilots. Amelia Earhart was the first president. Today there are over 6,000 members in the US, Canada and 35 other countries. The Canadian Ninety-Nines, part of the international organization, have a mission "to engage in educational, charitable and scientific activities and to provide a close relationship among women pilots and unite them in any movement that may be for their benefit or for that of aviation in general." The East and West Canada Sections were formed in 1950 and 1951 and now have 10 chapters with over 240 active members promoting safety through training and education.

CHAPTER

10

Risky Rescues and Tragic Losses

FOR DECADES, BUSH PILOTS HAVE fulfilled many roles, transporting passengers working in mineral exploration and mining, public health, recreation and tourism, firefighting and smokejumping. In so doing, especially in the days before radio and cellphones, pilots were the eyes and ears of the North. A bedsheet spread flat on the ground or a cross made of conifer branches on the ice signalled that any passing pilot should land if at all possible to offer assistance. At any time, a routine supply drop or forest patrol could turn into an emergency run where lives were at stake.

While bush pilots flew many diverse groups of people into remote regions, they also risked their lives on mercy flights to bring out ill and injured patients. The first known air-ambulance flight in northern Canada occurred on August 28, 1920. J.W. Thompson was flown from Moose Factory on James Bay to Cochrane, Ontario, by bush pilot William R. Maxwell, a former RAF captain, in a Curtiss HS-2L. Thompson had contracted an inner-ear infection that had spread to the mastoid bone behind the ear. Without a mastoidectomy, he could have lost his hearing or even his life. Later, Maxwell would become the first director of the Ontario Provincial Air Service (OPAS).

By the late 1920s and through the 1930s, such medical evacuation (medevac) flights became more common. The longest emergency medical flight lasted from November 27 to December 20, 1939, when W.E. Catton flew a Junkers W34 from Winnipeg to Repulse Bay, Northwest Territories, and returned with a man whose frostbitten hands had turned gangrenous. The first civilian air ambulance in North America was established after the Second World War by the Saskatchewan government to cover great distances and serve remote communities.

The man who would become known as "King of the Medevacs," Wilhelm Adolph "Willy" Laserich, was born in northeastern Germany. He arrived in Canada on board a Norwegian sealing boat in 1951 at age 19 and worked his way north. By 1957, he had earned his pilot's licence in Edmonton, then moved with his new wife Margaret Rose to Hay River and their first house, complete with outhouse. Before working as a pilot, Laserich picked up work as a diesel engineer in an ice plant where fish were frozen for air delivery south. Laserich earned his living as a bush pilot for 50 years and became a hero to residents in remote communities, where his trademark orange toque was a welcome sight.

From a base at Cambridge Bay, Laserich clocked over 40,000 hours in the air, the equivalent of circumnavigating the world 800 times. He conquered the most extreme weather and survived emergency landings at night and sinking into spongy muskeg. He took off when the only visual reference was the line left by the snowplow, only to rise up above the clouds into sunny skies. Laserich called it a risk, but a calculated one. "There's bad weather and there's dangerous weather, and up here it's critical you know the difference," he commented.

Once, after dropping 6,560 feet (2,000 metres) in mid-flight because an iced engine powered out, he calmly landed on a frozen lake. He flew Norsemen, Twin Otters and Beavers, ferrying dead bodies for funeral services, whale meat for feasts and prisoners for incarceration. He found injured hunters, stranded pilots and lost miners. But his hero status rested on the 5,000 medical evacuations he completed with a perfect safety record, including the transportation of a man whose arm had been torn off in a mining accident and packed in an ice-filled suitcase that accompanied him on the flight to hospital in Edmonton. When a bronchiolitis epidemic hit at Gjoa Haven, in present-day Nunavut, Laserich evacuated the children four at a time. When it spread to other communities, he flew 24/7 for two weeks. Then there were the happy trips—the six births on board.

In 1970, Laserich applied for an operating licence to operate a charter service out of Cambridge Bay. In spite of local support, his petitions were continually refused, but the government in Ottawa did pay enough attention to slap him with over 200 citations in 1977. He was cited for infractions such as accepting a meal from an elder after a medevac flight and not declaring the value of the food as income, and for flying in temperatures below -40°C/F. "It's -40 three months at a time!" Laserich protested. He faced over $1 million in fines and a year in jail.

On January 18, 1982, the longest and most expensive aviation trial in the North to that date came to a conclusion. Judge Frank Smith delivered his verdict to the court held inside the Cambridge Bay Hotel, which was packed with people who were alive thanks to Laserich's mercy flights. "He's the stuff of the bush pilots of old," Smith said. "He is supplying a service that he is uniquely qualified to perform." He found Laserich guilty of one count of running an illegal charter service, assigning a fine of $250 and giving him a lifetime to pay. When Laserich tried to settle his debt, it had already been paid. But legal fees had bankrupted him, so the following year, his three children pitched in and launched Adlair Aviation, since the operating licence had finally come through. Laserich was still branded an outlaw and troublemaker by government air-transport authorities, and his ongoing legal hassles spurred him to refer to himself and his crews as Willy's Bandits. Despite this, he was held in high regard in the Arctic communities he served. He never refused someone in need.

Bishop John Sperry, an Anglican minister in Kugluktuk in the 1950s and 60s, remembered when his wife Elizabeth, a midwife, was asked to accompany a pregnant woman to Yellowknife. Laserich flew in from Cambridge Bay to pick them up. It was pitch black and the weather was turning nasty. During the flight, Iris, the pregnant woman, went into labour. There was nowhere to land, so the baby was born in mid-air. Willy contacted air-traffic control to tell them to add an extra passenger to the manifest. In recognition of her in-flight birth, the baby was called Angel. Over the span of his flying career, five more babies were born with Laserich at the controls.

Willy Laserich died of heart failure in 2007, after being medevaced from Cambridge Bay to a hospital in Edmonton in his own Lear Jet. He was accompanied by his sons—René in the cockpit and Paul at his side. He was 75. Willy Laserich was inducted into Canada's Aviation Hall of Fame in 2010.

Laserich and other bush pilots undertook many incredibly risky rescues and mercy flights, but sometimes that wasn't enough. Para Rescue was initiated in 1942 by Wop May while he was in charge of No. 2 Air Observer School (2AOS) in Edmonton, as part of the British Commonwealth Air Training Plan. The city was on the northwest staging route between the US mainland and Alaska after the US joined the war in 1941. Many inexperienced pilots were called upon to fly over the challenging terrain. Mechanical failures, unpredictable weather and primitive navigational aids caused many "premature" landings. 2AOS participated in many northern mercy missions to find these missing aircraft and crews, often with unfortunate results. Wop May found this unacceptable and decided to do something about it. He began organizing an air-rescue team, the first formal para-rescue team in the world.

Team members would parachute into crash sites and administer first aid to the injured. Twelve volunteers stepped forward and received rudimentary training in how to jump from a plane and pull the D-ring handle on their chest-pack parachutes. They wore no reserve chutes, and wind drift was calculated by throwing an Eaton's store catalogue out the open door. During one of the first jumps, a parachutist plunged through the cloth wing of a parked aircraft. Obviously, more training was required. In early 1943, May dispatched two of his volunteers, Owen Hargreaves and Scotty Thompson, to the smoke jumpers school in Missoula, Montana, to be trained by the US Forestry Service. For six weeks, they studied the finer points of parachute operation, physical stamina, situational analysis, letdowns (how to release a parachute when you are hung up in a tree), proper body position exiting the plane and landing techniques. They returned home with their new skills and borrowed equipment to train two other volunteers. But May's para-rescue team needed proper facilities and that required military muscle. In

1944, Air Vice Marshal T.A. Lawrence, Commander of the North West Air Command in Edmonton, agreed to integrate this civilian rescue unit into the RCAF. The first course began later that year and included jump training, bush lore, wilderness survival, mountain climbing and medical aid. It was a tradition that grew through the decades, and in 1998, the Canadian Forces School of Search and Rescue (CFSSAR) was established at the Canadian Forces Base at Comox on Vancouver Island, BC.

Many downed pilots and their passengers have had reason to be grateful for the skills of search-and-rescue personnel, but not all searches for lost planes have a happy ending. "If I ever crash, they'll never find me," said legendary pilot Charles "Chuck" McAvoy. He was almost right. McAvoy and fellow pilot Daryl Browne had been ferrying American geologists over the central Arctic tundra in heavy snow and poor visibility. When McAvoy didn't land on schedule with the two geologists in his 1938 Fairchild 82, Browne set out in his Otter to look for him. It was June 9, 1964. With 10 years' flying experience under his belt, McAvoy had taken part in nearly all of the northern search-and-rescue missions, often finding downed pilots before the RCAF could. Now he was the focus of a desperate search. "I stayed awake 50 hours to search. That's the longest I've ever spent in my life without putting my head on a pillow. A lot of people were looking for him because he had found a lot of other people," Browne said.

Bush pilot Chuck McAvoy poses beside his aircraft in the Yellowknife area in 1960. LIBRARY AND ARCHIVES CANADA PA-176297

The hunt for McAvoy lasted for months. Local pilots and the RCAF flew round the clock, but nothing was found. It was as if the land or the network of lakes had swallowed him. For almost 40 years, his fate was one of Canada's aviation mysteries. It was even the subject of the 1973 "Ballad of Chuck McAvoy," written by Frank Ferguson and sung by Ted Wesley:

Now they tell you that Chuck McAvoy still flies his ghostly
plane,
Lookin' for a place to set her down.
When the fog is thick and misty in this cold and barren land,
You can hear his engine searchin' for the ground.

On August 3, 2003, a helicopter pilot flying for a mining company found wreckage, human remains and McAvoy's identification at a crash site near Lupin Lake on the Northwest Territories–Nunavut border. He was flying a crew of geologists back to a nearby camp when he thought he saw something in a jumble of rocks. Circling back and passing 200 feet (60 metres) directly above, he saw plane wreckage. Landing nearby to get a better look, the pilot saw that the downed plane was largely intact, and he speculated that McAvoy might have been attempting to land when he caught a skid and rolled. "It's camouflaged in the rocks pretty well," he said. "You've got to be close and if you're off a bit, you can't see it there. You'd just think it was rocks, it's blended in so well." McAvoy and his two passengers are believed to have died on impact.

Thirteen years before Chuck McAvoy vanished, the disappearance of bush pilot Johnny Bourassa had also launched an intensive search. After serving as an RCAF pilot during the Second World War, Bourassa returned home and delivered mail between Peace River and Fort Vermilion by horse and buggy in summer and dogsled in winter. In 1950, he was hired to fly a charter service from Yellowknife to Bathurst Inlet in a de Havilland Beaver. On May 18, 1951, Bourassa lifted off from open water heading northeast to the Salmita Mine gold find. He refuelled there and switched from floats to skis since his destination in the high Arctic was still frozen. At Bathurst Inlet, his supervisor told him to put in only the amount of fuel needed to return to the Salmita Mine fuel cache. It was expensive to restock northern caches, so pilots were instructed not to carry extra fuel back south. Bourassa did not want to stop at Salmita so he filled up and departed directly to Yellowknife. When the supervisor stopped at Salmita the next day, he saw Bourassa's Beaver floats and assumed he had crashed en route. He retraced the route to Bathurst but found nothing. There he learned Bourassa had fully fuelled his plane; the search area had just grown exponentially.

With full fuel tanks, the Beaver could fly from Bathurst to northern Saskatchewan or Alberta or into the Mackenzie Mountains. In the time before locator transmitters, searching for a missing aircraft by sight in the North was a long and often futile process. The search expanded to a few hundred miles on each side of the intended route from Bathurst to Yellowknife. Nothing was spotted, so the search was halted. Four months later, Bourassa's plane was located on Wholdaia Lake, 350 miles (565 kilometres) southeast of Yellowknife near the Northwest Territories–Saskatchewan border. It was on shore and intact except for a broken ski.

Inside was a note from Bourassa. He said he had mistaken Aylmer Lake for Lac de Gras, which put him east of Fort Reliance, after which he flew west until the treeline, believing he was then east of Snowbird or Ennadai Lake. Running out of fuel, he was forced to land on the soft ice of Wholdaia Lake which was weak and disintegrating or "rotten." He was going to walk south around the lake then on to Fort Reliance. He estimated it would take him three weeks to cover the 250 miles (400 kilometres).

If only he had made a different choice. Maps on board the Beaver showed it was about 125 miles (200 kilometres) to Fort Fond du Lac on Lake Athabasca and only 62 miles (100 kilometres) to Stony Rapids. If he had gone around the south end of the lake as the note said, he would have seen the Native portage trail, as wide as a wagon track, to Selwyn Lake and on to either Fond du Lac or Stony Rapids.

An aerial search would not locate one lone man on the vast landscape, so ground searchers were called in. The largest search ever undertaken by the Canadian Rangers, No. 7 Company, Yellowknife, began with the help of trappers from as far away as Edmonton. The bush between Wholdaia Lake and Fort Reliance was searched and searched again. No trace was found. No campsite. Nothing. Searchers concluded that Bourassa took a shortcut across the lake, counting the rotten ice would still hold. But the lake is dotted with small islands (aits) and underwater rocks that retain daytime heat and thaw the ice. It was a treacherous situation that could drown a man, and it could have taken the life of Johnny Bourassa.

When writer Farley Mowat was researching his book *People of the Deer*, Bourassa had flown him to remote Inuit locations. The 2003 Canadian adventure movie *The Snow Walker* is based on the Mowat short story *Walk Well, My Brother*, which tells of a bush pilot who is on his way to Yellowknife when his engine cuts out. He is forced to land on a frozen lake and then walk out. The sad tale of Johnny Bourassa could have been Mowat's inspiration.

CHAPTER

11

A Bird's-Eye View

BUSH PILOTS LIVE ON THE EDGE, but despite the risks, they love their bird's-eye view of the world. They are there for each other in good times and bad, and experienced pilots can quickly assess the skills of their peers and know who they want to fly with. Nothing can replace hours logged in the air, but successful bush pilots also need many other talents: advanced outdoor survival and first-aid skills; the ability to repair an airplane using little more than duct tape and wire; and knowledge of how their airplane performs in changing conditions over boreal forest, tundra, mountains and Arctic seas. They must also be well-versed in navigation, cockpit instrumentation and Canadian Aviation Regulations. Tom Lamb, Keith Olson, Walter "Babe" Woollett and Art Schade all proved they had the right stuff when they took to the skies over the unforgiving Canadian wilderness.

"Do not ask us where we fly, tell us where you want to go" was the motto of Tom Lamb and his six pilot sons, collectively known as the Flying Lambs. He started Lamb Airways Ltd. (later Lambair) in 1935 with one Stinson-Reliant SR8, a five-passenger plane with lots of cargo room that could be outfitted with floats, skis or wheels. He operated out of The Pas, 450 miles (725 kilometres) north of Winnipeg, which was a jumping-off point for the North. His first flights brought supplies into Moose Lake, where his father was a successful trading-post grocer.

Being a naturalist as well as a pilot, Lamb noticed that while he and the Cree lived in the midst of marshes with a large beaver and muskrat population, the animals themselves had few available passageways of any depth in which to swim and build their lodges. He undertook to dredge out parts of the marshland, re-establishing the original canals and waterways, dams and dykes. The irrigation ditches were inspected by foot in summer and on skates in winter, but patrols also could be done from the air by just looking down.

Lamb took out an ad in the local newspaper promoting his air services. Rivers had long been used as highways in the region, but flying was a means of avoiding dangerous rapids. He also turned his inventive mind to making bush flying easier. He developed special axles, so skis could be jacked up to keep them from freezing into the ground; a rubber bag that fit inside the cargo space, so freshly killed fish and animals would not drip blood in the plane; and heat vents in the walls instead of the floor, so perishable cargo would not spoil. Many Lamb flights carried doctors and medical staff from the National Health and Welfare Department, sent to vaccinate northern residents, set broken bones and fly out the most severely ill to hospital.

In 1946, Lamb flew internationally with beavers, but not in a Beaver aircraft. He babysat 10 pairs of Manitoba beavers en route to Montreal, then Miami and on to Buenos Aires, where they transferred to a Canso flying boat provided by the government of Argentina and then flown to Ushuaia in Tierra del Fuego, the world's most southerly town. There they were released to build new lodges in a marshy lake east of the Andes.

Tom Lamb died in 1969, and in 1970 the Manitoba government honoured his dedication to the northern wilderness and its wildlife by designating a 772-square-mile (2,000-square-kilometre) tract of land near The Pas as the Tom Lamb Wildlife Management Area. Lamb was inducted into Canada's Aviation Hall of Fame in 2009 for his exploration and development of northern Manitoba and the Arctic, mercy missions to aid First Nation peoples and his commitment to conservation.

While some pilots get hooked on the adrenaline and adventure of bush flying and never leave, others use it as a way to log the air time required for a commercial airline job. Keith Olson worked for six years as a bush pilot for

Tom Lamb, from 1959 to 1965 and tells many stories of his adventures during that time. Olson earned his private pilot's licence in Calgary in 1955, then an aeronautical engineering diploma, his commercial pilot's licence and, just for good measure, his mechanic's licence. Then he had to find a job. He applied to the Lambs in Manitoba and was hired after a 15-minute aerial demonstration in a Cessna 180 on skis. At first Olson flew short hauls to Moose Lake, then moved on to longer runs to Snow Lake and Thompson. Olson was sent out on his own for three months to work with an Indian agent "up north," soliciting new business flying cargo and customers wherever they wanted to go. One of the Lambs dropped in occasionally to pick up the roll of bills Olson accumulated in cash payments.

Every day presented Olson with new challenges. One rule of thumb was that people always had more stuff than the plane had room. Often the Cessna's doors had to be removed to load in a sleigh, supplies, dogs and a couple of trappers before flying a short distance. "A lot of work for almost nothing, but that's what you did," Olson recalled in an interview with writer Shirlee Matheson. "We called them 'trapper trips' and charged a 12-mile minimum." Sometimes Olson flew Native families to their traplines or picked up Native children from remote settlements to fly them to boarding school at Chesterfield Inlet and Churchill. Once he was contracted to fly mineral-staking prospectors to Gods Lake in northeastern Manitoba. It was spring and the lake's surface snow was melting. As soon as he touched down, Olson he knew he was in trouble. He cut the engine, and as soon as the plane stopped, his passengers jumped out wearing snowshoes. The plane had sunk so much they could rest their elbows on the wing tip. They spent the entire day tramping down the wet snow into a makeshift runway and digging out the skis before they could take off.

In 1961, Olson was assigned to a 14-month contract with International Nickel Company of Canada Limited (INCO) to supply their drilling camps around Thompson. Then he flew an army survey expedition that was correcting northern maps and transported Geological Survey of Canada employees who were trekking across the North as far as the Arctic Circle. "All that time we lived in fly-infested tents," Olson recalls, "or paddled a canoe while swatting mosquitos. The bugs just about drove us nuts. We sometimes had to wear head nets."

Olson graduated from flying the Cessna to an Otter and a Norseman; he liked them both: "The Norseman was a challenge to fly but it's a genuine bush plane. I also loved the single Otter. It would do what the Norseman would do but a lot better . . . The Otter could get off and land slower and in shorter distances. On floats it was able to carry a bit more than the Norseman, and it had good range."

Olson became more adept at flying on floats than on skis because there was more business in summer. "But you can get into a lot of trouble on floats because you can't just stop the airplane. You have to pick your water and estimate the wind and the current to know where you should be able to stop," he explained.

Olson spent his last four years with the Lambs flying out of Churchill, where the ocean was his landing and takeoff strip. He had to handle waves, tides, weather and reefs and also locate a secure place to tie up so his plane would not be carried out to sea. "Down south you have trees around the lakes and you can get into the sheltered side," he explained, "but there is no shelter up there because there are no trees—and no spare parts if the aircraft gets damaged." August was considered to have the best flying conditions, but even then large chunks of sea ice bobbing in the water near remote settlements like Igloolik on the Melville Peninsula threatened to smash the floats to pieces.

To make emergency repairs, Olson carried epoxy plastic body-filler similar to that used on cars. In cold weather, he had to use a blow pot to warm the engine and encourage it to start. "We carried brooms to brush snow off the wings then we'd prop them up in front of the engine to hold the tarp from going right against the cowling and put weights around the edges to keep the heat in. The gas fumes inside were suffocating. Maybe that's why pilots age fast!"

Nor was fashion a concern. To keep warm, Olson bought a quality parka with a fur-lined hood, quilted nylon air-force wind pants and air-force war-surplus flying boots inside of which he wore two pairs of socks and leather slippers. On top of all this he added industrial one-piece coveralls and a down-filled jacket. With this attire he was ready to fly and keep warm should his plane be forced down. He never had a co-pilot, but sometimes he hired a similarly dressed "helper" who lived in The Pas. "In winter we had to dig out our gas drums from caches in a snowdrift and roll them out. It involved a lot of physical work using shovels or whatever we could find." And performing toilet functions when overnighting at a remote winter location presented major logistical problems. "In those days you hardly ever had to go, because you never drank anything. You didn't want to have go to the bathroom," Olson recalls. "You had to remove the one-piece coveralls if you were going to do any serious necessaries."

Olson claims he was never lost, but once he was "temporarily disoriented" flying some schoolteachers in the Norseman on a five-hour trip to Baker Lake from Churchill. The weather was stormy with poor visibility, but if he got to Baker there was a beacon and he could land nearby. But he could not pick up the beacon in the bad weather, so he turned in the direction he felt was the coast and eventually recognized the area between Whale Cove and Eskimo Point (now Arviat). From there, he thought he could make the settlement at Rankin Inlet, and his passengers agreed to go for it. They made it with just a few sips of gas left. After seven hours rattling around inside the Norseman, the occupants were "just vibrating."

After his six years with the Lambs, and with a family to support, Olson looked for a change of scene and more regular hours. When he'd started flying the Cessna, he was grossing $240 a month with his room and board included. When he left, he was making $1,000 a month and was paid by the flying hour: $4 an hour south of Churchill and $5 north, plus base pay. Most commercial airlines at the time paid on a cents-per-mile basis. In 1965, the Olson family moved to Winnipeg, where Olson was employed for a year by Transair flying scheduled runs to northern communities in a Beech 18, then in larger DC-3s and Cansos. One day when Olson was wondering if that was all his future held, a friend at the Winnipeg Flying Club told him Air Canada was hiring pilots. He had never thought of them. Olson called, got a job and stayed there until retirement.

Walter "Babe" Woollett was another bush-pilot natural who eventually made the transition to a large airline. Woollett was born in England and got his nickname because he was the youngest in the family. He served in the RAF from 1924 to 1929, then came to Canada and became a bush pilot with the Fairchild Aerial Surveys at Lac-à-la-Tortue, Quebec. His monthly salary of $250 was an amazing sum at the time. Woollett joined Canadian Airways in late 1930 as a flying mailman airlifting mail from Saint-Hubert, Quebec, to Saint John, New Brunswick, by following the railroad line. His first run did not get off to an auspicious start. His engine conked out three times, and each time he had to set down and fix it. The next year, Woollett transferred to the winter airmail run along the North Shore of the St. Lawrence, throwing mailbags out over a number of villages by aiming at a flag planted in the snow. In 1934, Canadian Airways had the monopoly to supply towns in the Chibougamau goldfields area, and they hired Woollett to fly out of Senneterre, Quebec, in a Fairchild 82 (CF-AXB) doing a job he described as "shuttling back and forth with equipment, food supplies, booze and people of every description including members of the oldest profession."

In the winter of 1935–36, Woollett's aircraft was caught in a blizzard and damaged ("pranged," as he called it) during a rough landing on a frozen river in northern Quebec. Expecting rescue, he put on the snowshoes he kept in the rear and tamped out a landing strip in the snow for his rescuers. But nobody showed up. After five days, the irritated Woollett stomped out the following message in big letters with his snowshoes: LAND HERE YOU BASTARDS. He and his aircraft were finally located and retrieved, and the grumpy Woollett continued bush flying, doing aerial mapping as well as medical rescues.

During the Second World War, Woollett worked with the British Commonwealth Air Training Plan, overseeing schools in Quebec and Ontario. He received the Order of the British Empire (OBE) for this service. Appointed superintendent of the eastern division of Canadian Pacific Airlines after the war, he worked with Grant McConachie developing the company's Pacific passenger network. Woollett died at his home in Hawaii in 1998 and was inducted into Canada's Aviation Hall of Fame in 2003.

Henry Arthur "Art" Schade epitomized the resourceful bush-pilot pioneers who handled all risks and delivered the goods. On a Christmas Eve mail run in 1933 north of Sioux Lookout in western Ontario, Schade was heading to the tiny settlement of Goldpines, which had started out as a tent camp clustered around an HBC post and served as home to gold prospectors working at Red Lake and their families, as well as a stopping place for prospectors during the gold rush of the late 1920s. Soon it grew to include three stores, three restaurants, a hotel, barbershop, post office, bank, law office, pool hall and tavern. The population fluctuated between 100 and 130 permanent residents and about the same number of transients. During the winter, frozen waterways served as landing strips but the thickness and smoothness of the ice could never be guaranteed.

Like every other small, remote community, Goldpines depended on bush planes for mail and Christmas packages. Everything was ordered early by mail from catalogues, and all incoming parcels and letters were stored at the Sioux Lookout warehouse ready to be flown to Goldpines. Then everyone waited for the lake to freeze. And they waited. The ice was not thick enough for a ski landing but was too solid for a floatplane landing. On December 24, Art Schade received word the ice was thick enough for his plane with all its packages to land.

Flying over the area, Schade saw a small Gipsy Moth plane already on the ice and decided to put down nearby.

Everything looked good, and there was even a welcoming party of villagers standing on shore with their arms in the air. But everything was not okay. The Moth was stuck in a layer of melting ice and could not break free to take off. Schade did not know this, and there was no radio communication to tell him. He thought that the people waving their arms were welcoming him, not warning him not to land. He landed his big Bellanca only to immediately start sinking through the ice with scarcely enough time to jump out of the cockpit. His plane and all its cargo were soon submerged. Then the weather turned very cold, and everything was locked under a rapidly forming sheet of thick ice.

Not to be denied their Christmas goodies, the people of Goldpines organized a salvage operation; for 10 days and nights, they kept fires burning where the plane had sunk in order to soften the ice. Next they rigged a makeshift pulley system to haul the imprisoned plane out of the lake and up onto shore. The soggy Christmas mail and gifts were handed over to the postmaster, who dried them out and forwarded them to the addressees. Celebrations were late that year, but with painted macaroni strings, feathers and foil from tobacco tins to decorate the tree, and wild game, stuffed partridge, berries and honey on the table, life was good. Schade still had to get his plane back in working order to fly home. This he managed to do. It was, after all, just part of bush flying.

Epilogue

THE LAST FLIGHT OF *La Vigilance* began on September 2, 1922, with pilot Don Foss and engineer Jack Caldwell at the controls of the Curtiss HS-2L flying boat that had been flown by Stuart Graham on what is considered the first bush flight in Canada. They were delivering gas from Remi Lake in northern Ontario to Lac Pierre, a 90-minute flight. On the return trip, they ran into heavy rain and decided to set down on a small lake to wait for the weather to clear, since they had only enough fuel for one run into Remi Lake. But it was a small lake only about a half-mile long. Getting back up would be problematic.

Foss mulled over his situation. On takeoff, *La Vigilance* probably wouldn't clear the trees that grew right to the water's edge. But he had to try. When the rain stopped, he floated over the lake looking for deadheads, then powered up for takeoff. In struggling to clear the trees, a wingtip hit

The original hull of Curtiss HS-2L flying boat *La Vigilance* was preserved by the Canada Aviation and Space Museum and is displayed next to a Curtiss HS-2L reconstructed from parts of three different HS-2Ls and marked as Laurentide Air Service G-CAAC, the original *La Vigilance* registration. L.D. CROSS

the water, and the flying boat cartwheeled. Caldwell was thrown out and thumped onto the wing. Foss, unconscious in the submerged cockpit, was rescued by Caldwell. After Foss regained consciousness, the pair hiked along a nearby river to a trapper's cabin, and the next day the trapper guided them to the railway at Fauquier. On a return mission a few days later to recover the downed HS-2L, it was declared a writeoff. Even the engine was scrapped.

And there *La Vigilance* remained, slowly sinking into the silt of the lake bed until 1967, when it was discovered by Kapuskasing businessman Don Campbell. Nobody knew the true identity of the HS-2L, but the Canada Aviation and Space Museum decided to retrieve and reconstruct it as historically representative of its type, since no others existed. In the salvage operation from what is now called Foss Lake, the true identity of the plane became clear.

In 1970, the longest restoration project ever undertaken by the museum began on the Curtiss HS–2L. The restoration was complex and time-consuming due to the size of the plane and the need to reconstruct a complete hull. Curators wanted to retain the recovered hull for historical purposes, but the water-soaked wood was not suitable for restoration. In 1986, an exhibit of the G-CAAC *La Vigilance*'s original hull and a reconstructed HS-2L aircraft assembled from three different HS-2Ls was unveiled at the Canada Aviation and Space Museum in Ottawa, where it can be seen today. This is the only complete HS-2L in the world.

Some Museums with Bush Plane Holdings

Alberta Aviation Museum, Edmonton, Alberta
www.albertaaviationmuseum.com/

British Columbia Aviation Museum, Sidney, British Columbia
www.bcam.net/

Canada Aviation and Space Museum, Ottawa, Ontario
www.aviation.technomuses.ca/

Canada's Aviation Hall of Fame, Wetaskiwin, Alberta
www.cahf.ca/

Canadian Bushplane Heritage Centre, Sault Ste. Marie, Ontario
www.bushplane.com/

Canadian Warplane Heritage Museum, Mount Hope, Ontario
www.warplane.com/

Reynolds-Alberta Museum, Wetaskiwin, Alberta
history.alberta.ca/reynolds

Western Canada Aviation Museum, Winnipeg, Manitoba
wcam.mb.ca/

Selected Bibliography

Boer, Peter. *Bush Pilots: Daredevils of the Wilderness*. Edmonton: Folklore Publishing, 2004.

Braun, Don C., and John C. Warren. *The Arctic Fox: Bush Pilot of the North Country*. Boston: Back Bay Press, 1994.

Bungey, Lloyd M. *Pioneering Aviation in the West*. Surrey, BC: Hancock House Publishers, 1992.

Cole, Dermot. *Frank Barr: Bush Pilot in Alaska and the Yukon*. Portland: Alaska Northwest Books, 1986.

Erickson, George. *True North: Exploring the Great Wilderness by Bush Plane*. Guilford, CT: The Lyons Press, 2002.

Foster, J.A. *The Bush Pilots: A Pictorial History of a Canadian Phenomenon*. Toronto: McClelland & Stewart, 1990.

Gibson Sutherland, Alice. *Canada's Aviation Pioneers: 50 Years of McKee Trophy Winners*. Toronto: McGraw-Hill Ryerson Ltd., 1978.

Grant, Robert S. *Bush Flying: The Romance of the North*. Surrey, BC: Hancock House Publishers, 1995.

Godsell, Philip H. *Pilots of the Purple Twilight: The Story of Canada's Early Bush Flyers*. Calgary: Fifth House Ltd., 2002.

Keith, Ronald A. *Bush Pilot with a Briefcase*. Toronto: Doubleday Canada Ltd., 1972.

Lamb, Bruce. *Outposts and Bushplanes*. Surrey, BC: Hancock House Publishers, 2005.

Main, J.R.K. *Voyageurs of the Air: A History of Civil Aviation in Canada, 1858–1967.* Ottawa: Canada, Department of Transport, Queen's Printer, 1967.

Matheson, Shirlee Smith. *Flying the Frontiers.* Vol. II. Calgary: Detselig Enterprises, 1996.

McCaffery, Dan. *Bush Planes and Bush Pilots.* Toronto: James Lorimer & Co., 2002.

Oswald, Mary. *They Led the Way.* Wetaskiwin, AB: Canada's Aviation Hall of Fame, 1999.

Payne, Stephen, ed. *Canadian Wings: A Remarkable Century of Flight.* Vancouver: Douglas & McIntyre, 2006.

Spring, Joyce. *Daring Lady Flyers: Canadian Women in the Early Years of Aviation.* Lawrencetown, NS: Pottersfield Press, 1994.

———. *The Sky's the Limit: Canadian Women Bush Pilots.* Toronto: Natural Heritage Books, 2006.

Terpening, Rex. *Bent Props and Blow Pots.* Madeira Park, BC: Harbour Publishing, 2006.

Turner, Dick. *Wings of the North.* Blaine, WA: Hancock House Publishers, 1976.

Zuk, Bill. *True-Life Adventures of Canada's Bush Pilots.* Toronto: James Lorimer & Company Ltd., 2009.

Index

Acknowledgements

As with every work, there are numerous inputs, influences, interpretations, experiences, additions, deletions and events that meld to produce the final text. However, I would particularly like to thank Lesley Reynolds for her editing expertise and Bob Mercier for his help with research, as well as Marcia Rak of the Canada Aviation and Space Museum Archives, and Dora Winter of Library and Archives Canada for their assistance in sourcing documentation and illustrations in their collections.

About the Author

L. D. Cross is an Ottawa writer and member of the Professional Writers Association of Canada (PWAC), the Canadian Authors Association (CAA) and the Creative Non-Fiction Collective (CNFC). Her business and lifestyle articles have appeared in Canada and the US. Her publication credits include magazines such as *WeddingBells, Home Business Report, Legion Magazine, Profit Magazine, enRoute, AmericanStyle, Fifty-Five Plus, Health Naturally, Antiques!, Airborn* and *This Country Canada* as well as the *Globe and Mail* newspaper.

Her creative non-fiction has been recognized by the International Association of Business Communicators (IABC), Ottawa Chapter, EXCEL Awards for features and editorial writing, as well as the National Mature Media Awards for her articles about seniors. In 2011, her book *The Underground Railroad: The Long Journey to Freedom in Canada* received the inaugural Ontario Historical Society Huguenot Award honouring "the best book published in Ontario in the past three years which has brought public awareness to the principles of freedom of conscience and freedom of thought." She is also a co-author of *Inside Outside: In Conversation with a Doctor and a Clothing Designer* and *Marriage is a Business.*

More Amazing Stories by L.D. Cross

Code Name Habbakuk

A Secret Ship Made of Ice

L.D. Cross

print ISBN 978-1-927051-47-4
ebook ISBN 978-1-927051-48-1

By late 1942, Britain was desperate to win the Battle of the Atlantic. German U-boats had sunk hundreds of Allied ships, and Prime Minister Churchill had to find a solution to the carnage. Eccentric inventor and amateur spy Geoffrey Pyke proposed an invincible secret weapon: immense aircraft carriers built of ice that would roam the mid-Atlantic to protect Allied convoys from predatory U-boats. This is the fascinating story of the rise and fall of Project Habbakuk and how the British Royal Navy, the National Research Council of Canada and a workforce of conscientious objectors tested the strange concept in the Canadian Rockies.

Visit heritagehouse.ca to see the entire list of books in the Amazing Stories series.

More Amazing Stories by L.D. Cross

Treasure Under the Tundra

Canada's Arctic Diamonds

L.D. Cross

print ISBN 978-1-926936-08-6
ebook ISBN 978-1-926936-10-9

It is said that the sparkle from Canadian diamonds mimics the magnificent and seductive radiance of the northern lights. Yet until 1991, no one thought diamonds could even be found in Canada—no one except Chuck Fipke and Stu Blusson, who uncovered diamond-rich kimberlite in the Barrens at Point Lake in the Northwest Territories. Their spectacular find caused great excitement in international diamond circles and sparked the largest claim-staking rush in Canada since the 1896 Klondike gold rush. Here is the dramatic tale of two determined geologists who risked all and triumphed over incredible odds.

Visit heritagehouse.ca to see the entire list of books in the Amazing Stories series.